KONOS COMPASS

An Orientation to Using KONOS

Carole Thaxton
Jessica Hulcy

KONOS, INC.
RICHARDSON, TEXAS

We have as our ambition to please Him.

2 Cor. 5:9

DEDICATION

The KONOS COMPASS is dedicated to home-schooling families who are faithfully planting seeds in the hearts of their children.

ACKNOWLEDGEMENTS

Once again, we want to thank our wonderful families. It is for Jason, Jordan, Rhett, Jared, C.J., and Carson that the KONOS Curriculum was written. Without them there would be no KONOS. In the process of writing, these kids have been "guinea pigs" (experimenting with what we have written), "owls" (offering wise advice), "moles" (digging in as proofreaders, computer consultants, baggers, dishwashers, etc., etc., etc.), and "gophers" (encouraging us to "go-fer-it!").

Not many husbands would willingly and even cheerfully stay up all night proofreading, travel 200 miles looking for the right computer program, fly on a moment's notice to a national conference, and *want* their wives to have a ministry like ours. May God richly bless Charles Thaxton and Wade Hulcy! We appreciate them more than they could possibly know.

KONOS CURRICULUM happened because of many people. Hundreds of positive responses from our readers have encouraged us to keep plodding on, far beyond our natural strength. They have assured us of God's plan in our efforts, inspiring us to write a full elementary school curriculum and have given suggestions on how to better help families use KONOS. Our KONOS Counselors have been of particular help.

Special thanks goes to the families with whom we have co-oped. Ann Foster, Billie Miller, Connie Reese, Margaret Kunkel, Jan Sparks, and Joy Burkinshaw have taught what we have written, have helped us refine our ideas, and have prayed for us.

Connie Breyer, an experienced elementary school teacher, edited Volume I and wrote the daily lesson plans in the KONOS COMPASS. Cindy Barnett wrote most of the Inquisitive: Weather Unit and sections of Inquisitiveness: The Earth.

Ideas not expressed on paper would be of no help to families. It is because of the work of Herb and Laurie Pilz, Diana Pollock, and Shawn Montgomery, our faithful word-processors, that KONOS CURRICULUM is in finished form. Thanks also to Paul Lewis, Robert Morgan, and others who have helped with computer graphics and to Charlene Sims and the others at The Master's Press, who print our volumes. A very special thanks goes to C.J. Thaxton, who designed the front cover.

Most especially we thank our dear Father, who has loved us so much and has given us the most surprising resources to accomplish His work.

CONTENTS

BECAUSE...

WHAT?

WHAT IS KONOS?

KONOS is a Christian core elementary curriculum written by two home-schooling moms for home-schooling families. Using the unit studies method, KONOS teaches Bible, science, social studies, art, music, literature, health and safety, writing composition, and practical living under the unit themes of biblical character traits. These units are designed for family use. This means all the children can study the same topic at the same time instead of being sent to separate rooms to study separate topics. Because many of the activities are hands-on or discovery, children not only enjoy learning but also retain more of what they have studied. KONOS provides structure yet leaves plenty of flexibility for individual families to make the curriculum fit their family, instead of their family fitting the curriculum.

WHAT ARE THE DISTINCTIVES OF KONOS CURRICULUM?

1) Character training emphasis

KONOS agrees with Dr. Raymond Moore that the primary need of young children is character development. Young children hang on to stories of people and their character. This is why KONOS uses both B.C. and A.D. people as examples of each character trait. While studying Resourcefulness, we read about resourceful people such as Abigail, who lived before Christ and the inventor Eli Whitney, who lived after Christ.

We do not simply TELL our children to BE patient. We give them the opportunity to practice patience in the Patience unit by baking bread and waiting for it to rise, by planting seeds and waiting for them to grow, and by standing in line and waiting their turn. The lives of historical people serve as character models for our children. The activities give opportunity to practice the character trait. These help a child to internalize the character trait, making it a part of his own life.

2) Unit studies based on Biblical character traits

Unit studies is a teaching method that integrates all subjects under one theme. KONOS uses biblical character traits as the focal point of each unit.

To teach the unit theme of Self-control, KONOS has the children study the lives of Peter and Daniel (Bible, Character); read, memorize and write poetry (literature, language arts); learn many different dances (P.E., dance); sing rounds and songs with harmony (music); read about famous orators and practice delivering their speeches (social studies, speech); learn how man's voice box works (science); and, for one month practice controlling their tongues by speaking only words of praise and controlling their appetites by keeping a chart of their eating habits (practical living).

All the subjects are studied, but more importantly, the children have practiced controlling themselves (tongues, emotions, appetites, and bodies). All of the subjects point back to the biblical character trait. Children soon realize that dance coordination, rhyming verse, and

5

musical harmony are not merely subjects; they are vehicles for practicing godly chracter traits such as self-control.

3) Multi-leveled, family-oriented learning with all children studying the same topic

While most curricula are written for a classroom of thirty children of the same age, KONOS is written for a family with less (usually!) than thirty children of varying ages, levels, and abilities. If the unit of Attentiveness is studied, for example, all the students read about Samuel and how he heard the Lord calling him in his sleep. Six-year-olds might dramatize Samuel's story, while nine-year-olds retell the story. In the meantime, thirteen-year-olds write a quick synopsis of the story or search the Scriptures for other attentive people.

Under Attentiveness we also study the ear and the eye. Together the children dissect a cow's eyeball . After identifying the parts of the eye, the first-grader draws a picture of the eye labeling the parts he knows and tells how the eye works. The seventh grader and the fourth grader also take apart an old camera. The fourth grader then writes a paper either on how the eye works or how the camera works. The seventh grader writes a comparison paper on how the eye and the camera work.

While studying the ear, older children read about the ear and then set up an "ear" through which their younger siblings can crawl (a blanket over a table forms the ear canal, a real hammer striking a real piece of metal and touching another piece of metal simulates the stirrup and anvil, a sea shell with water in it forms the cochlea). Everyone learns together as a family while older children practice parenting, attentive to the needs of their younger brothers and sisters. In every KONOS unit, family members do some activities together. Then younger children do other more basic activities while older children do activities at higher levels (e.g., researching and writing reports).

4) Hands-on, experiential, participatory learning

While studying the biblical character trait of Resourcefulness, KONOS does not merely study the lives and inventions of the inventors; rather KONOS activities call for working with gears, building an electric generator, and constructing a telegraph. Children are not forced to memorize that Michael Faraday developed the first electrical generator and then ask, "Mommy, what's a generator?" They understand what the invention is because they built it themselves. They also have a greater appreciation for the resourcefulness of Faraday.

5) Discovery learning designed to produce thinking Christians

Discovery learning is one of KONOS' most important distinctives. Other curricula tell children information from a book or from a teacher's mouth and then ask them to regurgitate it back for a test. The best available curricula teach information and then ask the child to apply what he has learned. Discovery learning, on the other hand, doesn't tell children anything. Rather it asks them to figure it out on their own.

When we study Patience and bake bread, we ask the children to make a baker's hat for an art project. Rather than providing explicit instructions on how to make the hat, we hand them a picture of a baker's hat and say, "How would you make a baker's hat? Let's see what you come up with in an hour." We then leave them alone to figure it out. "But I can't" is a common first response. As his coach, you help your child to face the problem and not panic. We direct you with questions to ask him like "What shape is it?," "What material will you need?," "Where can you find help?" You will help only enough to get him started. It is amazing what children can do on their own. Only through challenges like this will they learn how to solve problems. However, many parents will not let their children figure things out for themselves. They are afraid they will make a mistake, or waste time, or make too much of a mess. But if we really want to produce thinking Christians, we parents must put on our gags and handcuffs. Jordan who measured his head circumference and sewed a baker's hat that sat on top of his head will never again forget a seam allowance.

Some years ago our children "built their own world" outlining the continents with yarn while crawling on their hands and knees in the backyard. "I'll never forget the shape of North America!," exclaimed C.J. The more children get totally involved in the learning process, the more likely they will remember what they have learned and be able to use it later. KONOS is full of thought-provoking discovery activities from "create your own plant classification system" to "figure out what a bird eats based on the shape of its beak." This is why KONOS produces thinkers.

WHAT DOES KONOS MEAN?

KONOS is the Greek word for "cone." The inverted cone symbolizes God at the top of all creation and all knowledge.

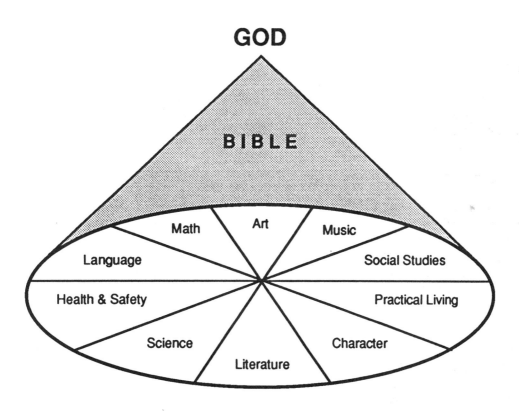

He reveals His character to us in His Word and through His creation. The more we study subjects with the enlightenment of the Scriptures and the Holy Spirit, the better we see God and His character through the world around us. It is God's character we seek to emulate. He is the source of both what we should know and what we should be. As we grow in godly character, we become more like Him, and in so doing, glorify Him.

IS KONOS BIBLE-BASED?

Yes, everything is taught from a Biblical perspective. Since Scripture was given to us for "instruction, reproof, correction, and training in righteous living," we weigh all we study against the Scriptures. Children need to understand God's standards. How can we expect a child to be honest in business if we never instruct him on what God says about this? How can we expect him to respect other people if he does not understand how God made people worthy of respect? The first step in becoming good is to recognize goodness. God is good and is the standard for all we teach.

Each character trait that we study is based upon the Bible, the standard for all truth. We take a look at God's description of what a righteous person is. We learn what the Scriptures teach about a particular character trait. As we study topics within that character unit, we use the Bible (like a flashlight) to shed light on the topic. When studying the solar system, we read and discuss the origin of the world and God's consistency in upholding the world. When studying the family, we look at biblical principles of how God created the family to be.

It is the job of us parents to both practice and teach each character trait. As we do, we illuminate our child's understanding of it and show what godly character really is. For our young children we are the interpreters and guides of the Scriptures, holding the flashlight to focus on a particular subject. Gradually ("line upon line, precept upon precept") and quite naturally, the children grow in understanding and internalize what they learn. When our children are in junior high and high school, we go through the whole Bible chronologically. At that point they are abstract thinkers, ready to understand and apply specific historical and moral principles. The long-range goal is to have children that will be able to discern from God's point of view.

WHAT GRADES DOES KONOS TEACH?

KONOS was written to cover what children should know in grades K-6. However, in preparing the comparisons of KONOS with state requirements and with a typical course of study used in textbooks, we realized that KONOS does, in fact, cover K-8. If you use KONOS with junior high students, you might want to include additional subjects like a foreign language, typing, instrumental music, and sports. Some families have successfully used KONOS with high school students as well. They merely read higher level books. For high school students carefully examine what is required in your state and augment appropriately. (See **DOES KONOS MEET STATE REQUIREMENTS?**)

WHAT IS INCLUDED IN KONOS?

KONOS CHARACTER CURRICULUM contains three volumes, each providing more than two years' worth of material for students K-8.

KONOS CHARACTER CURRICULUM
VOLUME I

Attentiveness • Obedience • Orderliness
Honor • Trust • Stewardship • Patience

KONOS CHARACTER CURRICULUM
VOLUME II

Inquisitiveness • Responsibility • Generosity
Courage • Wisdom • Loyalty

KONOS CHARACTER CURRICULUM
VOLUME III

Determination • Self-Control • Cooperation • Honesty
Initiative/Resourcefulness • Joy/Cheerfulness

Each unit includes lesson objectives; weekly lesson plans; Bible verses and biblical people to study; vocabulary words to use for vocabulary, spelling, and handwriting; library books (listed by grade-level) and other resources to borrow for the unit; plus multitudes of stimulating activities from which to choose. Each volume has a corresponding KONOS KIDS' TIMELINE (purchased separately). The Timeline package includes colorful, laminated figures of all the people who are studied in that volume. As the children study each person, they put the figure on the history line.

KONOS CHARACTER CURRICULUM is a complete curriculum when other phonics, math, and upper level language arts programs are added. All science, social studies, art, music, literature, health and safety to meet state requirements are covered. The KONOS Overview on the succeeding pages shows a sampling of what is included in each subject within each unit.

KONOS OVERVIEW · VOLUME I

ATTENTIVENESS

	BIBLE	HISTORY/SOCIAL STUDIES	SCIENCE/MATH	HEALTH/P.E.	PRACTICAL LIVING	ARTS/CRAFTS	MUSIC	LANGUAGE/LITERATURE	FIELD TRIPS
GENERAL	Prov. 20:12 Jesus Samuel			Attentiveness games	Paying attention				
EARS/SOUND/MUSIC	Prov. 4:20 Prov. 25:12 Is. 55:3	Helen Keller Anne Sullivan Alexander Graham Bell Antonio Stradivari	Ear parts and function Sound Telephone	Deafness Hearing test			Musical instruments Orchestra Dynamics Rhythm Tempo	Ear books Sound books Instrument books Helen Keller biography Listen	Ear doctor Sound studio Symphony Deaf school
EYES/SEEING	Mt. 6:22 Mt. 13:16-17 Lk. 6:41	Louis Braille John Dalton	Eye parts and function Braille	Eye exam Color blindness Nearsightedness/ Farsightedness Blindness		Drawing		Eye books Louis Braille biography	Eye doctor
OTHER SENSES	Gen. 3:3 Lk. 24:39 Jn. 20:27		Senses			Finger painting		Senses books	
FRONTIERSMEN/ TRACKING/ TRAPPING	Eph 5:15 Is. 55:3 Mary/Martha	Louisiana Purchase Westward Expansion Daniel Boone Davy Crockett Lewis & Clark Sacajawea Kit Carson Jim Bridger Jedediah Smith Brigham Young John Sutter	Animal tracks Compass/Orienteering Hunting/Trapping Animal furs	Wilderness hiking		Coonskin cap Buckskin shirt Moccasins Powder horn	Frontiersmen songs	Frontiersmen books Last of the Mohicans	Taxidermist
PREDATOR/PREY	Prov. 20:12		Predators/prey Animal camouflage & protection	Hunting/Fishing			Hunting songs	Tale of Jemima Puddle Duck "The Spider and the Fly"	Wilderness area
INDIANS	Prov. 20:12	Famous Indians		Indian campout Archery		Pottery Navajo weaving Jewelry Totem poles Headdress Masks Beadwork Cornhusk crafts	Indian dances	Hiawatha	Indian reservation
BIRDS	Mt. 6:26		Bird identification Bird parts, functions, behavior			John James Audubon Sketching birds Origami Bird feeder		Bird Books The Nightingale The Ugly Duckling Wheel on the Chimney Make Way for Ducklings	Zoo aviary Local park Duck pond

KONOS OVERVIEW · VOLUME I

OBEDIENCE

	BIBLE	HISTORY/ SOCIAL STUDIES	SCIENCE/MATH	HEALTH/P.E.	PRACTICAL LIVING	ARTS/CRAFTS	MUSIC	LANGUAGE/ LITERATURE	FIELD TRIPS
AUTHORITY/LIGHT	Jer. 26:13 Prov. 6:20-22 Col 3:20 Eph. 6:1 Heb. 13:17 Rom. 13:1-6 I Pet. 2:13-17 I Tim. 2:1-4 Jesus Abraham Joshua Noah Adam/Eve	Leaders/Authority figures Corrie Ten Boom Sir Thomas More	Light	Flashlight tag	Obedience to authorities	Insignias Candles	"I am the Light of the World"	Lighthouse books The Hiding Place	
BIBLE	II Tim. 3:14-17 Ps. 119 Timothy Sword drills	Johann Gutenberg Christian martyrs			Obedience to God's Word	Calligraphy Printing	"This Little Light of Mine" "The B-I-B-L-E"	The Bible	
KINGS & QUEENS	Ps. 47 Heb. 13:17 Mt. 25:21 I Pet. 2:17-20 Jesus King David Queen Esther Paul	Famous kings and queens Medieval Period		Jousting Fencing Chess Juggling		Royal costumes Knight costume Sword Jester costume Castles Coat of Arms Tapestry Medieval feast	Minstrels	Kings and Queens books Sword in the Stone Connecticut Yankee in King Arthur's Court The Boy's King Arthur Ivanhoe Robin Hood Nursery rhymes	
MILITARY	Mt. 8:5-10 II Tim. 2:3,4	Military heroes		Boot Camp Bivouac Marching drills		Military uniforms	Marches Bugle taps	Military hero books The Diary of Anne Frank	Recruiting center Military base
FRICTION-RESISTANCE	Rom. 12:2 Jesus Gideon		Force/Friction	Ice-skating Tug-o-war Sliding				Friction books	
HORSES	Ps. 32:9 Prov. 22:6 Job 39:19-35	Col. Alois Podhajsky Cowboys Pony Express	Horse breeds, horse parts, horse markings, tack	Horseshoes Horseback riding Rodeo Polo Lasso Pony express	Submissive behavior	Drawing and painting horses Frederic Remington Hobby horse Leather branding Cowboy tie	Cowboy songs "William Tell Overture"	Horse books Black Beauty Black Stallion Brighty of the Grand Canyon King of the Wind Misty of Chincoteague A Horse Named Justin Morgan The Man from Snowy River "The Village Blacksmith" Cowboy Small National Velvet	Rodeo Polo Horse races Riding stable
CONSEQUENCES OF DISOBEDIENCE	Heb. 12:5-11 Adam/Eve Hophni/Phineas David/Absalom David/Uriah Eli/sons				Behavior Point System			The Tale of Peter Rabbit The Poky Little Puppy The Story about Ping Corduroy Curious George books	

KONOS OVERVIEW • VOLUME I

OBEDIENCE (CONT.)

	BIBLE	HISTORY/ SOCIAL STUDIES	SCIENCE/MATH	HEALTH/P.E.	PRACTICAL LIVING	ARTS/CRAFTS	MUSIC	LANGUAGE/ LITERATURE	FIELD TRIPS
ACTION-REACTION	Gal. 6:7 Lot's wife		Newton's Third Law		Consequences of behavior				
CRIME AND PUNISHMENT	Ex. 21:24 Gal. 6:7b Rom. 13:1-4 Deut. 5:7-21 Jonah 10 Commandments	Court system Famous trials	Common math "crimes"		Family rules	Wall hanging Traffic signs		Laws and trials books Macbeth Inherit the Wind To Kill a Mockingbird Common language "crimes"	Court Police station

KONOS OVERVIEW · VOLUME I

ORDERLINESS

	BIBLE	HISTORY/SOCIAL STUDIES	SCIENCE/MATH	HEALTH/P.E.	PRACTICAL LIVING	ARTS/CRAFTS	MUSIC	LANGUAGE/LITERATURE	FIELD TRIPS
CREATING	God Gen. 1 Ps. 95 Ps. 98 Ps. 104 Ps. 148 David Solomon		Creation/Evolution	Creative dance	Creative cooking Creative wardrobe Table setting	Process of creating Varieties of media Photography	"This Is My Father's World" "How Great Thou Art" "All Things Bright and Beautiful" Composing music	An Artist A Family All Things Bright and Beautiful Story-writing	Art museum Craft fair
PLANNING/ SEQUENCING	I Cor. 14:40 Noah (Gen. 6:14-22) Zerubbabel (Ezra)	Famous people throughout history Geneology	Ancestry Housebuilding		Making plans Family geneology	Mazes		Noah's Ark Geneology books House construction books	Construction site Factory
COUNTING/ MEASURING	Num. 1:2 Num. 3:40 Ezra 8:34	Charles Babbage	Counting Measuring	Counting and measuring games Treasure hunt	Sewing	Jewelry-making		Counting and measuring books "Arithmetic"	Post Office Variety store
CLASSIFYING	I Kings 20:1 Noah (Gen. 6:5 - 8:29)		Sorting/Classifying Fractions		Home management Table setting Wardrobe coordination				
ANIMAL CLASSIFICATION	Gen. 1:25 Adam (Gen. 2:19) Noah	Aristotle Lamarck Linnaeus Darwin	Animal Classification			Mobile Prints Sculpture Puppets		Animal books Animal stories and poems	Zoo Wild Animal Park
PLANT CLASSIFICATION	Gen. 1:12	Linnaeus	Plant classification Tree identification Flower identification			Stencils Leaf press Collage Bookmarks Placemats Photography Potpourri Paperweight Pressed flowers Decoupage		Plant books Tree books	Nature walk Nursery
ROCK CLASSIFICATION	Ps. 24:1a Ps. 104:5a Job 28:1-10		Geology Rock classification Minerals/Crystals			Display cabinet Stone sculpture		Rock and mineral books	Rock hunting Jewelry store Gem cutter
REGULARITY/ DISCIPLINE	I Cor. 14:40		Scientific method		Personal discipline Habits				
SOLAR SYSTEM	Ps. 104:19-20	Kepler Galileo Newton	Sun Planets Moons Gravity Centrifugal force	Circle dances				Astronomy books	Observatory Planetarium
CALENDARS/ SEASONS	Eccl. 3:1-8 Gen. 8:22 Ex. 20:8-11 Mk. 2:27	History of calendars	Calendars Time Seasons Holidays		Cooking projects for every season	Crafts for every season	Seasonal songs	Seasonal poems and plays	

KONOS OVERVIEW • VOLUME I

TRUST

	BIBLE	HISTORY/SOCIAL STUDIES	SCIENCE/MATH	HEALTH/P.E.	PRACTICAL LIVING	ARTS/CRAFTS	MUSIC	LANGUAGE/LITERATURE	FIELD TRIPS
DECEPTION/ILLUSION	II Thess. 2:3 Deut. 11:16 II Jn. 1:7a Prov. 13:20 Deut. 18:9-11 Prov. 3 Satan Eve/Satan David/Saul Samson/Delilah Ruth/Boaz/Naomi	David Copperfield Samuel Morse	Optics Optical illusion	Avoiding abuse and deception	Baking Choosing good companions	M.C. Escher drawings Magic tricks, costumes, staging Costumes, masks, make-up		Chanticleer and the Fox The Gingerbread Man Hansel and Gretel Little Red Riding Hood The Wolf and the Kids Snow White and the Seven Dwarfs Pinocchio Magic and disguise books Code books Codes	Wig shop Costume shop Magic show
GOD'S TRUSTWORTHINESS	Ps. 22:5 Prov. 3:5 Heb. 11 Abraham Daniel Shadrach, Meshach, Abednego Job John the Baptist Noah David Joseph	Corrie Ten Boom Israel's history			Prayer		Hymns	The Hiding Place The Chronicles of Narnia The Tanglewood's Secret	
GOOD SHEPHERD/SHEEP/WEAVING	Is. 53:46 I Pet. 2:25 Ps. 23 Jn. 10	Shepherding	Sheep			Weaving projects Carding Spinning Dyeing wool	Hymns	Charlie's New Cloak Pele's New Suit A Shepherd Looks at the Twenty-third Psalm A Child's Look at the Twenty-third Psalm And Now Miguel Sheep and weaving books	Sheep farm
FAITH IN GOD	Phil 4:6 I Pet. 5:7 Ps. 56:3,4 Mt. 6:25-34 Elijah	George Mueller Jim Eliot Hudson Taylor John Bunyan	"Faith" in physical laws	Worry/Anxiety Fears/Phobias			Hymns	Pilgrim's Progress	
FLOATING AND SHIPS	Ps. 46:10 Ps. 65:5-7 Ps. 107:23-32	Robin Graham Thor Heyerdahl Robert Fulton Historic boats	Buoyancy Surface tension Boats	Life-saving and water safety Swimming/Floating Boating Surfing Water-skiing		Model boats Drawing boats	"Row, Row, Row Your Boat" Sailing songs	Kon-Tiki Treasure Island Boat books	Marina Canoe trip
FLIGHT AND AIRPLANES	Ps. 55:6	Pilots and astronauts	Air Flight Airplanes Rockets Flying animals	Rings/Trapeze		Air painting Kites Model airplanes Mobile	"Let's Go Fly a Kite"	Twenty-one Balloons Around the World in 80 Days Riders on the Wind Airplane and rocket books Biographies of pilots and astronauts	Airport Helicopter ride Hot air balloon

KONOS OVERVIEW · VOLUME I

PATIENCE

	BIBLE	HISTORY/SOCIAL STUDIES	SCIENCE/MATH	HEALTH/P.E.	PRACTICAL LIVING	ARTS/CRAFTS	MUSIC	LANGUAGE/LITERATURE	FIELD TRIPS
PLANT GROWTH/GARDENING	Eccl. 3:1-8 Ps. 147 Mt. 7:15-23 Mt. 21:18-22 Mt. 12:33-37 Mt. 13:31-32 Mt. 17:20 Gal. 6:7-8 Gal. 5:22-23 Rom. 11	Luther Burbank George Washington Carver	Plants (parts, functions) Trees Flowers Reproduction Cross-breeding Grafting Identification	Poisonous plants	Gardening	Flower arranging Dried flower crafts Leaf-rubbing and stencils Seed crafts Potpourri	Plant songs	Plant poems Plant and gardening books Biographies of Burbank and Carver	Garden Nursery Art museum
GRAIN/BREAD/YEAST	Jer. 5:24 Ruth/Boaz/Naomi Ex. 16:1-7 Lk. 22 Jn. 6 Deut. 8:3 Mt. 4:1-4 The Lord's Prayer Ex. 12 (Passover)	Sir Alexander Fleming U.S. farming regions Breads around the world	Farming/Farm tools Grains Yeast/Fungus/Mold Volumes Fractions	Wheat allergy Fungus diseases	Bread baking Sewing	Tea party	"The Farmer in the Dell"	Little Red Hen Farming books Yeast, fungus, mold books Baking books	Farm Farm equipment store 4-H Club Bakery Grocery store
HUMAN BIRTH/GROWTH	Lk. 2:40 I Pet. 22 Heb. 5:11-14 I Cor. 3:1-11 Ps. 104:21 I Cor. 13:11-12 Jr. 3:1-21 Seed carriers of Christ Birth and rebirth	Babies Stages of development Elderly persons Relatives	Human reproduction Abortion Childbirth Stages of development	Baby safety Growth charts Growth abnormalities Diseases of old age	Baby and child care	Baby gifts	Musical production for nursing home	Leo the Late Bloomer Jamie's Turn Reproduction/birth/growth books	Obstetrician Playground Toy store Nursing home
ANIMAL BIRTH/GROWTH	Ps. 37:7	Jane Goodall Chinese silk production	Reproduction Caterpillars/Butterflies Insects/Spiders Frogs/Toads Birds/Eggs Fish/Eggs Mammals			Critter cage Butterfly paintings Melted wax paintings Pysanky egg decorating Eggshell mosaic Animal prints	"Bullfrogs and Butter-flies" "If I were a Butterfly"	Horton Hatches an Egg Egg-hatching books Caterpillar/Butterfly books Insect/Spider books	Nature museum Fish hatchery
WAITING CONSTRUCTIVELY	Jas. 5:8 Mt. 6:27 Is. 40:31 Joseph Jacob Job David	Easter		Family games	Practical waiting skills	Easter banner Easter bonnet	"Coming again"	A Little at a Time McElligot's Pool	

KONOS OVERVIEW · VOLUME I

	BIBLE	HISTORY/ SOCIAL STUDIES	SCIENCE/MATH	HEALTH/P.E.	PRACTICAL LIVING	ARTS/CRAFTS	MUSIC	LANGUAGE/ LITERATURE	FIELD TRIPS
STEWARDSHIP									
GENERAL	Jas. 1:17 Gen. 1:27-30 I Cor. 10:31 Daniel					Stewardship cone	Hymns		
STEWARDSHIP OF THE BODY									
NUTRITION	Dan. 1 Ps. 104:14 Prov. 23:20-21	Foods around the world	Foods Herbs and spices	Nutrition Bean bag games "Fruit-basket Turnover"	Meal planning Reading labels Food shopping Cooking Serving Herb garden Herbal tea party Co-op dinner	Table decorations Assorted food crafts (collage, sculpture, jewelry, wreaths, etc.)		Nutrition books Cookbooks	Health food store Butcher shop Cafeteria Dietician
EXERCISE	Phil. 1:20 Rom. 12:1	Kenneth Cooper	Muscles	Fitness tests Jumping rope Biking Group games Calisthenics Aerobics	Family exercise program	Physical conditioning course		Exercise and fitness books	Aerobic class Fitness center Conditioning course
REST	Ps. 127:2 Ex. 20:8-11 Mk. 6:31 Mk. 2:27 Sabbath Jesus Mary Magdalene Mary, mother of Jesus Johanna Salome		Sleep	Rest/Sleep Insomnia	Sabbath rest	Restful art	Lullabies and other restful music	Hush Little Baby All the Pretty Horses Rest and sleep books	
FUN	Prov. 17:22 Prov. 15:13, 15, 30 Eccl. 3:4 Ps. 126:2, 3	Comedians Circus Clowns Bill Cosby Emmett Kelly Ringling Brothers		Recreation	Jokes/Riddles Games/Hobbies	Hobbies Puppet show Circus	Funny songs	Joke and riddle books Funny poems Clown and circus books	Circus Family fun excursion
ABUSE/PREVENTION	Rom. 12:1 Rom. 6:12, 13 I Cor. 6:20 Paul	Nurses/Doctors Dentists Mayo brothers Clara Barton Florence Nightingale Linda Richards	Disease Teeth	Medical care Dental care Smoking Alcohol/Drug abuse Sexual abuse	Preparing for adoles- cence	Uniforms Medical equipment Ambulance		Disease/Doctor/Hospital books Teeth/Dentist books Biographies of doctors and nurses Smoking/Alcohol/Drug abuse books	Pharmacy Doctor's office Hospital Hospital supply store Uniform store Ambulance Dentist Orthodontist Alcoholics Anonymous

KONOS OVERVIEW · VOLUME I

	BIBLE	HISTORY/SOCIAL STUDIES	SCIENCE/MATH	HEALTH/P.E.	PRACTICAL LIVING	ARTS/CRAFTS	MUSIC	LANGUAGE/LITERATURE	FIELD TRIPS
STEWARDSHIP OF MONEY AND POSSESSIONS									
MANAGING MONEY AND POSSESSIONS	Lk. 16:10 Mt. 6:19-21 Parable of the talents The widow's mite The rich young ruler Joseph	International coins and bills Richest people Banking/Credit Larry Burkett	Money		Shopping Budgeting/Tithing	Papier maché bank Budget box		Money/Banking books	Coin collector Bank
STEWARDSHIP OF TALENTS									
CAREERS	Col. 3:17 Col. 3:23 I Pet. 4:10 Lk. 19:13 Dan. 1,2	Occupations Finding and preparing for jobs Missionaries Malla Moe David Livingstone William Carey Isobel Kuhn Hudson Taylor Adoniram Judson Wilfred Grenfell			Using our talents/abilities	Pantomime Talent show	Hymns Composers	Career books Biographies of missionaries and other Christians at work	Mall Town Nursing home
STEWARDSHIP OF TIME									
MEASURING AND TELLING TIME	Ps. 90:12	History overview of the world	Time Clocks		Family projects	"Hickory, Dickory, Dock" craft Playwriting	Time songs	Tenses (past, present, future) Time and clocks books	Clock shop
BUDGETING TIME	Eph. 5:16 Ps. 90:12 Solomon				Personal priorities Scheduling time	Assignment book		Time organizers	
STEWARDSHIP OF NATURAL RESOURCES	Ps. 8:4-9 Gen. 1:28 Ps. 12:15:16	Environmental Protection Agency Park rangers Teddy Roosevelt John Muir	Natural products Ecology/Conservation Erosion	Fire prevention Air pollution Water treatment	Recycling Compost pile Conserving energy	Painting signs	"For the Beauty of the Earth" "This Land Is My Land" "This is My Father's World"	Don't You Dare Shoot that Bear! The Stone Cutter Biographies of Roosevelt and Muir Conservation books	Nature hike Camping trip Soil testing clinic Wildlife sanctuary or game preserve Water treatment plant

KONOS OVERVIEW · VOLUME I

HONOR

	BIBLE	HISTORY/ SOCIAL STUDIES	SCIENCE/MATH	HEALTH/P.E.	PRACTICAL LIVING	ARTS/CRAFTS	MUSIC	LANGUAGE/ LITERATURE	FIELD TRIPS
ATTRIBUTES OF GOD	Is. 6:3 Rev. 1:8 Eccl. 12:14 Ps. 95:3-5 Rev. 19:6 God's character	St. Augustine	Power		Activities to demonstrate God's attributes		Hymns	Theology books What's in an Egg? Three in One	
POTTERY/ SCULPTURE	Is. 64:8 Job 43-6 Rom. 9:20-24 Idols	Sculptors Statue of Liberty Mt. Rushmore						The Stone Cutter	Potter's studio China shop
TABERNACLE	Exod. 25-40 Lev. 10:3 Tabernacle Offerings Priests Sacrifice of Jesus		Oils Spices			Play dough Modeling dough Sculpture Carving	"The Little Light of Mine"	The Tabernacle of God in the Wilderness of Sinai The Book of Life: Vol. 4	
CATHEDRAL/ CHURCH ARCHITECTURE	Ps. 2:11 Mt. 18-20 Ps. 150:1	Filippo Brunelleschi Sir Christopher Wren	Science of construction			Symbols in art Tabernacle Priest costume	"The Church's One Foundation" "Green Cathedral" Handbells	Cathedral books The Hunchback of Notre Dame	Cathedral Gothic church Handbell choir
REVERENT BEHAVIOR/HYMNS	Deut. 6:5 Ps. 29:2 Ps. 95:6 Ps. 34:1 Ps. 100:4 II Chron. 7:14 Ps. 147:1 Ps. 149:1 Mary David Moses Paul Hophni/Phineas Cain/Abel/Seth	Hymn writers Fanny Crosby Isaac Watts Charles Wesley John Newton			Church dress and behavior Worship	Cathedral architecture Stained glass	Hymns Spirituals Hymn composition Choreography	Hymnbooks	
HEREDITY/ INDIVIDUALITY	Gen. 1:24 Gen. 1:27-28 Ham/Shem/Japheth	Gregor Mendel Races Individuality of persons			Inherited traits		"I am a Promise" "If I Were a Butterfly"	Many examples of individuality in literature	Airport or other public place
COUNTRIES/ CULTURES	Lev. 19:34	Countries/Nationalities	Heredity/Genetics		Ethnic cooking National sports National traditions	Self-portrait	Ethnic songs and dances	Stories from and about various countries	Ethnic restaurants and shops
BLACK MOVEMENT	Gen. 1:27 Gen. 9 Gal. 3:28	Black movement Civil rights Martin Luther King, Jr. Harriet Tubman Famous Afro-Americans	Natural resources	Inherited diseases National sports	Overcoming prejudice	Ethnic crafts	See Africa in Vol. II: Inquisitiveness – Geography/Continents	Roll of Thunder, Hear My Cry Roots Biographies	Afro-American museum
KINDNESS/SERVICE/ ETIQUETTE	Pet. 2:17 Mt. 7:12 Mt. 25:34-45 Jn. 5:12 Jn. 13:14 Rom. 15:1 Gal. 6:2 Jas. 3:9-10 Jesus The Good Samaritan	Mother Teresa William Booth Charitable organizations			Serving one another Courtesy			Manners books Biographies	

KONOS OVERVIEW · VOLUME II

INQUISITIVENESS

	BIBLE	SOCIAL STUDIES	SCIENCE/MATH	HEALTH/P.E.	PRACTICAL LIVING	ARTS/CRAFTS	MUSIC	LANGUAGE/ LITERATURE	FIELD TRIPS
RESEARCH/ REFERENCE	II Tim. 2:15 Prov. 18:15 Prov. 22:17 II Tim. 3:16-17 Hos. 4:6 Bereans (Acts 17:11) Solomon (2 Chron. 1:10,11)	Francis Schaefer John Dewey (Dewey Decimal System) Library of Congress Nobel Prize winners	Nobel Prize	Public health research	Bookmobile for shut-ins Using catalogues Using Yellow Pages Interviewing Study skills	Library floor plan		Curious George Library/reference/ research skills Alphabetizing Bible reference books Writing questions	Library
SCIENTISTS/ SCIENTIFIC METHOD	Eccl. 7:25 Prov. 15:14 Rom. 1:19, 20 Mt. 6:26-34	Aristotle Copernicus Kepler Galileo Newton Bacon Other famous scientists	Logic Reasoning skills Scientific method/Experiments Light/Shadow Circles/Angles Pendulum Telescope		Superstitions False knowledge Reasoning games (e.g. Chess, Stratego) Science fair	Dramatizing Bacon's life Pendulum art "Art in a Box" Drawing with ellipses (ovals) String design art Painting rainbow	Songs to pendulum rhythm	Biographies of famous scientists Light and shadows books Circles and angles books	Clock shop Science fair
GEOGRAPHY/ CONTINENTS	Gen 1:2, 9,10 Ps. 24:1,2 Ps. 89:11 Ex. 20:11	Earth Science Geography Continents/Cultures	Map skills	Geography games		"Build the World" "Earth Pillow"	"This is My Father's World"	Geography and map books Books about continents Representative books for each continent Journaling	
WEATHER	Jer. 10:13 Prov. 30:4 Jer. 14:22 Ps. 65:9-10 Prov. 25: 13-14 Job 38	Adm. Beaufort Louis Fahrenheit Anders Celcius Benjamin Franklin	Weather Weather instruments Measuring temperature/ wind velocity Forecasting	Kite flying Sledding	Predicting and preparing for weather	Finger painting Watercolor painting Weather vane Other wind machines	Weather songs	Books about weather Many weather poems (e.g., "The Cloud," "The Wind")	Weather station
EXPLORERS/ NAVIGATION/ SAILING	Ps. 19 Rom/ 11:33, 34 Job 9:9 Ps. 147:4 Gen. 1:28	Leif Erikson Marco Polo Christopher Columbus Vasco de Gama Ferdinand Magellan Hernando Cortez Other famous explorers	Stars Constellations Magnetism/Compass Navigation Geometry of a circle (angles, degrees) Sailing/Ships	Sailing Health and disease of explorers Explorer games	Constellation cookies Gingerbread baking Rope-splicing Knot-tying	Star crafts Cross-staff Astrolabe Carving Viking ship Viking helmet/shield/ sword "Fake" marble Sketching ships Model sailboat Mural Aztec crafts Dramatization	"Seek Ye First the King-dom of God" Sailing songs	Books about navigation and sailing Carry On Mr. Bowditch Poems about sailing and stars Winnie the Pooh Biographies of explorers Play-writing	Exploration hike Sailing Night watch Planetarium Crew race Oriental rug store Oriental craft store
DETECTIVES	Mt. 7:7	Arthur Conan Doyle F.B.I and private investigators	Forensic medicine	"Hide and Seek" "I Spy" "Hide the Thimble"	"Clue" Finger-printing	Finger-print art		Books about detectives and crime-fighting Sherlock Holmes and other detective stories Mysteries Writing mystery stories	Police station Forensic lab

KONOS OVERVIEW · VOLUME II

RESPONSIBILITY

	BIBLE	SOCIAL STUDIES	SCIENCE/MATH	HEALTH/P.E.	PRACTICAL LIVING	ARTS/CRAFTS	MUSIC	LANGUAGE/LITERATURE	FIELD TRIPS
GENERAL	Gen. 1:28 Deut. 6:5 Prov. 3:9-10 Deut. 12:26-28 I Sam. 15:22 Prov. 19:16 Mt. 6:33 Mt. 12:50 Prov. 20:4 Ex. 20:3 Prov. 3:5-6 Ex. 20:12 Prov. 1:8-9 Eph. 6:1 Lev. 19:18 Jn. 13:3-5 Mk. 10:15	Jobs requiring responsibility			Our responsibilities to God, to parents, to others Daily chores Work skills	Poster Dramatization	"Lazy Mary, Will You Get Up?"	Horton Hatches an Egg Mike Mulligan and His Steam Shovel The Little Red Hen Keep the Lights Burning, Abby Little Toot "A Psalm of Life"	Construction site
PET CARE	Gen. 1:26-28 Gen. 9:2 Ps. 8 Prov. 12:10		Pets	Prevention and treatment of pet diseases	Choosing and caring for a pet	Stuffed animals Sculpture Pet houses Pet parade	"How Much Is That Doggy In The Window?"	Books about pets Pet stories Pet poems The Cricket in Times Square Beautiful Joe Writing pet stories	Pet store Obedience training school Veterinarian
BEAVERS		Beaver trappers	Beavers	Holding breath Swimming	Being "busy as a beaver"	Poster Model of beaver lodge		Books about beavers Beaver stories	Beaver pond Haberdashery
ANTS	Prov. 6:6-9		Ants	Disease-carriers	Being responsible without being asked	Drawing Ant crafts	"The Ants Go Marching" "High Hopes"	Books about ants The Ant and the Grasshopper	Ant colony Picnic
EARLY SETTLERS	Gen 1:28 Prov. 12:11 Prov. 12:24 Prov. 12:27 Prov. 13:4 Prov. 6:10-11 Prov. 24:30-34	Jamestown Capt. John Smith Pocahontas Powhatan John Rolfe Plymouth William Brewster Edward Winslow Susannah Winslow John & Francis Billington Miles Standish William Bradford John Carver Samoset Squanto Massasoit New York Peter Minuit Peter Stuyvesant Massachusetts Bay John Winthrop John Endicott New Hampshire Maryland Lord Baltimore		Diseases and treatments in early America Colonial games Ice skating	Living like the early settlers (lodging, cooking, dress, work, play, worship) Thanksgiving feast Corn husking or apple-paring party Cleaning	Drawing Model fort Dramatization Bead-stringing Whittling Thanksgiving play Centerpieces Doll house	"Now Thank We All, Our God" "Twenty-third Psalm"	Books about early settlements and colonies Biographies Pocahontas Landing of the Pilgrim Fathers "The Village Blacksmith" "Courtship of Miles Standish" Writing first person stories Writing and news release	Jamestown Plymouth Plantation

KONOS OVERVIEW • VOLUME II

	BIBLE	SOCIAL STUDIES	SCIENCE/MATH	HEALTH/P.E.	PRACTICAL LIVING	ARTS/CRAFTS	MUSIC	LANGUAGE/ LITERATURE	FIELD TRIPS
EARLY SETTLERS (CONT.)		Rhode Island Roger Williams Ann Hutchinson Connecticut Thomas Hooker Delaware New Jersey Carolinas Pennsylvania William Penn Georgia James Oglethorpe			Log cabin model				

KONOS OVERVIEW · VOLUME II

LOVE/GENEROSITY

	BIBLE	SOCIAL STUDIES	SCIENCE/MATH	HEALTH/P.E.	PRACTICAL LIVING	ARTS/CRAFTS	MUSIC	LANGUAGE/LITERATURE	FIELD TRIPS
GENERAL	I Cor. 13 Jas. 1:17 Lk. 6:38 2 Cor. 9:7 Acts 20:35 Phil. 23, 4 Widow's mite Beatitudes	Valentine's Day Charitable organizations	Money math	Games and prizes for needy kids	Meaning of love Loving one another Loving the unlovable	Greeting cards Game boards	"Blest Be the Tie That Binds" "Seek Ye First"	Love poems Biographies Reading to shut-ins	Salvation Army Visiting the needy
CHRISTMAS	Jn. 3:16 Mt. 1, 2 Lk. 1, 2	Christmas customs around the world			Celebrating as a family Family traditions	Madonna and child paintings Many homemade Christmas gifts Baking Decorating Christmas cards	Handel's "Messiah"	Christmas poems and stories The Best Christmas Pageant Ever	Christmas shopping
EASTER	Matthew Mark Luke John Mk. 16:15	Jesus Easter customs Evangelists			Evangelism	Easter parade Pysanky eggs Marionettes Evangelistic puppet show	Easter songs	Easter stories Biographies	Evangelistic talk (e.g. Youth for Christ)

KONOS OVERVIEW • VOLUME II

	BIBLE	SOCIAL STUDIES	SCIENCE/MATH	HEALTH/P.E.	PRACTICAL LIVING	ARTS/CRAFTS	MUSIC	LANGUAGE/LITERATURE	FIELD TRIPS
COURAGE									
GENERAL	Deut. 31:6-7 Josh. 1:6-7 Joshua (Josh. 1-24) Elijah (I Kgs. 16-34) Hezekiah (2 Chr. 32) Shadrach, Meschach, Abednego (Dan. 3) Daniel (Dan. 6) Prophets Jeremiah (2 Kgs. 23-37; 2 Chr. 35-36; Jeremiah) Isaiah (Isaiah) Jonah (Jonah) David (I Sam. 17) Gideon (Judg. 6-8) John the Baptist Early Church (Acts)	William Tell Joan of Arc Martin Luther	Fire/heat Figuring odds (probability)	Fire safety	Foolish vs. courageous behavior Taking risks	Collage Dramatization Banner	"Shadrach, Meschach, and Abednego" "A Mighty Fortress Is Our God"	The Matchlock Gun Call It Courage David and the Giant The Courage of Sarah Noble Christian biographies Writing a log	Christian bookstore
AMERICAN REVOLUTION		Patrick Henry King George III Nathan Hale Samuel Adams Abigail Adams John Hancock Paul Revere William Dawes Samuel Prescott Minutemen General Howe General Clinton George Washington Henry Knox Thomas Jefferson Benjamin Franklin Thomas Paine Lafayette John Paul Jones Baron von Steuben Benedict Arnold Molly Pitcher	Geography of eastern U. S. Firearms	Obstacle course	Cooking hasty pudding and fire cakes	Battlesite model Mural Quill/Ink Soldering Tinsmithing Shadow box Flag	"Yankee Doodle" "My Hat It Has Three Corners"	Books about the Revolutionary War Biographies Johnny Tremain "Paul Revere's Ride" "Molly Pitcher" Famous speeches	Printer Silversmith Engraver Boston Lexington Concord Bunker Hill

KONOS OVERVIEW · VOLUME II

WISDOM

	BIBLE	SOCIAL STUDIES	SCIENCE/MATH	HEALTH/P.E.	PRACTICAL LIVING	ARTS/CRAFTS	MUSIC	LANGUAGE/LITERATURE	FIELD TRIPS
GENERAL	Proverbs Prov. 4:7 Prov. 9:13 Prov. 10:8 Prov. 10:17 Prov. 9:8-10 Prov. 8:33-34 Prov. 18:15 Prov. 21:11 Prov. 13:1 Prov. 6:20-23 Prov. 10:1 Prov. 17:21 Prov. 1:10-16 Solomon (I Kgs. 1-12) Abigail/Nabal (I Sam. 25) David (I Sam. 18-31 vs. II Sam. 11-13)	Wise people	"Wise" animals	Competitive games Being a referee	Making wise choices (habits, friends/ spouse, clothing) How to get wise Arbitrating/negotiating/ judging Contests	Mobile Paper dolls	"The Wise Man Built His House Upon a Rock" Many hymns	Teaching the Word of Truth The Wise Fool The Emperor's New Clothes Yertle the Turtle The Wind in the Willows Many other stories Figures of speech	
SAFETY	Prov. 14:15 Prov. 26:11	Red Cross	Pain	Household safety Traffic safety First aid	Maintaining a safe home Bicycle safety	Posters A safety play Traffic signs		Books about safety and first aid	Red Cross Bike hike
GOVERNMENT	Prov. 9:10 Prov. 12:15	George Washington Thomas Jefferson Benjamin Franklin Alexander Hamilton James Madison Dolly Madison U. S. Constitution Bill of Rights Parliamentary procedure Current affairs			Forming a club	Clubhouse Architecture of govern- ment buildings Block prints	Patriotic songs	Books about the U. S. Constitution Biographies Proverbs Acrostics Note-taking Newspapers/News magazines	Washington, D.C. Architecture walk
PRESIDENTS/ ELECTORAL PROCESS		Presidents Electing the president						Biographies	

KONOS OVERVIEW • VOLUME II

LOYALTY

	BIBLE	SOCIAL STUDIES	SCIENCE/MATH	HEALTH/P.E.	PRACTICAL LIVING	ARTS/CRAFTS	MUSIC	LANGUAGE/ LITERATURE	FIELD TRIPS
GENERAL	Jonathan Ruth/Naomi Mary Magdalene Rahab Judas Peter's denial	Loyal employees			Siblings Being a good friend	Greeting cards Memory books	"Auld Lang Syne" "Blessed Be the Tie That Binds"	Letter-writing Friend stories My Friend Obadiah Old Yeller The Incredible Journey	A friend's home
CITIZENSHIP	Rom. 13:1-7 Tit. 3:1 I Pet. 2:13-17	Citizenship U. S. history review Patriotic celebrations		Marching drills	"Fourth of July" or "I Love America" parade and party	Flag Cross-stitch "Birth of America" one-man show	Patriotic songs	Patriotic poems Man without a Country	

KONOS OVERVIEW · VOLUME III

COOPERATION

	BIBLE	SOCIAL STUDIES	SCIENCE/MATH	HEALTH/P.E.	PRACTICAL LIVING	ARTS/CRAFTS	MUSIC	LANGUAGE/ LITERATURE	FIELD TRIPS
SYSTEMS OF THE BODY	Rom. 12:4-8 I Cor. 12:12-26 Eph. 4:1-16	Medical professions Bubonic plague	Each system of the body Body parts and functions Measuring and ratios Graphs Microscope	Diseases (prevention and treatments) Fitness tests Gymnastics Games		Sculpting Drawing people		Anatomy and physiology books	Pharmacy Various doctors' offices Beauty salon Manicurist Blood bank
BEES	Gal. 6:10 Eph. 4:1-3 Col. 3:12-14 I Pet. 4:10		Bees		Cooking with honey	Beeswax candles and seals	"Flight of the Bumble-bee"	Bees books	Bee hive
STATES/REGIONS	Rom. 12:18 Rom. 14:19 I Tim. 2:1, 2	U.S. geography Civil War Abraham Lincoln Governor Senator	Natural resources of each region	Sports for each region	Cooking for each region	American art and crafts Crafts for each region	Patriotic songs Songs for each region	U.S.A. and states books Walk Across America Civil War books Roots	
TOWN/COMMUNITY	Rom. 12:18 Rom. 14:19 I Tim. 1:1, 2	City officers City geography/Maps City transportation			Neighborhood block party	Cityworker uniforms	"Who are the People in Your Neighborhood?"	Town and community books	Town tour Fire station
FAMILY/CHURCH	Gal. 6:10 Eph. 4:1-3 Col. 3:12-14 I Pet. 4:10 Peter/Paul Paul/Barnabas Church at Colossae	Church Family/Relatives Family tree		Cooperative games	Identifying spiritual gifts Working together Playing together	Cross-stitch Collage Mural	Harmonizing	Little Women	Local church

KONOS OVERVIEW • VOLUME III

HONESTY

	BIBLE	SOCIAL STUDIES	SCIENCE/MATH	HEALTH/P.E.	PRACTICAL LIVING	ARTS/CRAFTS	MUSIC	LANGUAGE/ LITERATURE	FIELD TRIPS
BOOKS	Prov. 12:17￼Phil. 4:8￼God	Famous authors￼Real, fictional, and legendary characters￼Brothers Grimm￼Hans Christian Andersen￼Dr. Seuss￼Beatrix Potter	Book printing		Discerning truth from falsehood	Costumes￼Puppetry￼Book writing, illustrating and publishing		Books about books￼Aesop's Fables￼Stories by the Brothers Grimm￼Stories by Hans Christian Andersen￼Beatrix Potter books￼Classics to Read Aloud to Your Children￼Perelandra	Library￼Typesetter￼Printer￼Bindery
NEWSPAPERS AND OTHER MEDIA	Eph. 4:25￼Prov. 12:17￼Prov. 24:28￼Prov. 25:18￼Exod. 20:16￼Ps. 68:11￼Prophets and false prophets	Famous journalists￼Freedom of the Press	Weather map￼Stock reports￼Math from classified section		Typing￼Selling	Political cartoons￼Comics￼Photography￼Lay-out￼Broadcasting		Books about newspapers￼Newspapers￼Magazines￼Newswriting	Newsstand￼Newspaper printing office
BUSINESS AND ADVERTISING	Prov. 11:1￼Prov. 20:10￼Prov. 20:23￼Prov. 12:22￼Eph. 4:25￼Eph. 4:28￼Jas. 5:12	Famous businessmen￼History of money and banking￼Capitalism	Math￼Money￼Bookkeeping￼Bank accounts, tax, insurance￼Honest salesmanship		Starting and managing a business honestly￼Product assembly	Engraving￼Trademarks￼Ads		Books about business and advertising￼Biographies of famous industrialists￼Business letters and resumes	Local stores￼Ad agency￼Businesses￼Bank
GENERAL	Prov. 12:19￼Prov. 12:22￼Prov. 21:6￼Prov. 24:28￼Col. 3:9, 10￼Eph. 4:25, 28￼Mal. 1:14, 3:8￼Micah 6￼I Jn. 1:5-10￼Jesus vs. Peter￼Levi￼Satan				Truth-telling vs. lying	Posters￼Drama	Hymns	Ali Baba and the Forty Thieves￼Sam, Bangs, and Moonshine￼Pinocchio	Polygraph test

KONOS OVERVIEW · VOLUME III

DETERMINATION

	BIBLE	SOCIAL STUDIES	SCIENCE/MATH	HEALTH/P.E.	PRACTICAL LIVING	ARTS/CRAFTS	MUSIC	LANGUAGE/LITERATURE	FIELD TRIPS
GENERAL	Heb. 12:1 Eph. 6:18 I Tim. 6:11,12 Jer. 1:17 Prov. 10:4 Paul's journeys Stephen Thessalonian church				Goal-setting Completing projects	Posters	"I Have Decided to Follow Jesus"	The Little Engine That Could The Tortoise and the Hare Where the Red Fern Grows The Incredible Journey	
OLYMPICS AND PHYSICAL SKILLS	I Tim. 6:12 II Tim. 4:7 Heb. 12:1 I Cor. 9:24-27 Paul Stephen	Ancient and modern Olympics Olympic champions			Sports skills Re-enactment of ancient Olympics			Olympics books Biographies of Olympic champions Chariots of Fire	
HANDICAPS	Phil. 4:13 Eph. 3:16,21 Eph. 6:10 Rom. 15:1 Ps. 18 Paul	Handicapped people		Handicaps	Helping the handicapped			Books about handicaps Biographies of handicapped people Joni	Prosthetic technician Physical therapist Occupational therapist Learning Center
GREAT FEATS	Lk. 1:37 Phil. 3:13-14 Tower of Babel	Famous engineers and builders Famous bridges, tunnels, dams, canals	Bridges Tunnels Dams Canals			Model bridges, tunnels, dams, canals Mechanical drawing	"London Bridge" "Erie Canal" "Climb Every Mountain"	Books about great feats	Concrete manufacturing site Road-building site Bridges Tunnels Dams
EXPEDITIONS	Heb. 12:1 Phil. 3:13-14	Polar explorers Mountain climbers Underwater explorers	Polar regions Mountains Sea life/Aquarium	Hiking Mountain climbing Fishing Snorkeling SCUBA diving	Cooking fish	Stuffed animals Shell craft Sponge art Various fish crafts		Polar books Mr. Popper's Penguins Mountain climbing books Underwater books 20,000 Leagues under the Sea Full Forty Fathoms	Ski shop Night hike Zoo Aquarium Fish market Pet store
ATOMIC RESEARCH	Heb. 11:3 Heb. 12:1	Atomic researchers	Basic chemistry Atomic research Radioactivity	Radiation exposure	Kitchen chemistry	Solar print		Chemistry books Biography of Marie Curie	University chemistry lab Radiologist Nuclear power plant

KONOS OVERVIEW · VOLUME III

SELF-CONTROL

	BIBLE	SOCIAL STUDIES	SCIENCE/MATH	HEALTH/P.E.	PRACTICAL LIVING	ARTS/CRAFTS	MUSIC	LANGUAGE/LITERATURE	FIELD TRIPS
BODY/APPETITES	Prov. 29:11 Gal. 5:22,23 I Pet. 5:8 II Pet. 2:19 II Pet. 3:17 II Tim. 2:4 Lk. 12:35 I Cor. 16:13 I Pet. 2:1 Eph. 5:18 I Cor. 10:13 Col. 3:8-17 Eph. 6:10-20 I Pet. 1:13-25 Peter Daniel James Samson	John Newton Personalities/temperaments	Hunger Thirst Sexual urge	Alcohol/Drug abuse Sexual temptations Good and bad habits	Cooking Fasting	Armor (Eph. 6:10-20)		_Christians You Should Know_ _Why Wait_ _Preparing for Adolescence_ "The Road Not Taken"	
DANCE	Rom. 12:1-2 I Cor. 6:19-20 Ps. 149:3 Ps. 150:4 David	Ballet and other dances Ethnic groups and their dances		Body movements to songs Folk dance Ballroom dance Ballet lessons Tap dance Ice skating Jumping rope Marching drills	Appropriate body movement Folk dancing with family friends	Calligraphy Tutu Set design Program design	Songs with body movements Ballets	Dance books Ballet Stories _The Nutcracker_ Biographies of ballet dancers	Liturgical candle Ballet Ballet class Leotard store
EMOTIONS	Prov. 16:32 Eph. 4:26, 27 Mt. 14:27 Jesus	Jackie Robinson	Facial muscles		Handling emotions	Dramatization	Feelings in music	Emotions books _Charlotte's Web_ Biography of Jackie Robinson Emotional poems Figures of speech	
POETRY	Psalms David	Famous poets		Rhythm Jumping rope	Poetry reading circle	Dramatizing poems Drawing	Rhythm	Rhymes Poetry reading, analyzing, writing Simile/metaphor Biographies of poets	Library
SPEECH	Eph. 5:4 Eph. 4:29-32 Jas. 1:26 Prov. 15:1 Prov. 17:14 Prov. 25:11 Jas. 1:19 Prov. 10:19 Prov. 28:13 Jesus	William Jennings Bryant Abraham Lincoln Patrick Henry Martin Luther King, Jr. John Kennedy Demosthenes Cicero Jonathan Edwards Ventriloquists Ethel Barrett Dialects/accents	Speech/Voice		Speech development of family members Poor speech habits Telephone manners Building up one another with positive speech	Ventriloquism/dummy Drawing, mounting, framing		Famous speeches and sermons Foreign languages Common grammatical mistakes Public speaking Biographies of great speakers	Children's center Public place

	BIBLE	SOCIAL STUDIES	SCIENCE/MATH	HEALTH/P.E.	PRACTICAL LIVING	ARTS/CRAFTS	MUSIC	LANGUAGE/ LITERATURE	FIELD TRIPS
SINGING	I Chron. 16:23 II Chron. 20:21 II Chron. 29:30 Ps. 47:6-7 Is. 12:5 Col. 3:16 David	Famous singers			Family sing-along Recital		Varieties of songs Vocal training Intro. to opera Praise songs	Songbooks Opera Stories Biographies of famous singers	Singer(s)

KONOS OVERVIEW • VOLUME III

INITIATIVE/ RESOURCEFULNESS

	BIBLE	SOCIAL STUDIES	SCIENCE/MATH	HEALTH/P.E.	PRACTICAL LIVING	ARTS/CRAFTS	MUSIC	LANGUAGE/ LITERATURE	FIELD TRIPS
GENERAL	Col. 1:29 Mt. 7:7-11 Mt. 6:33 Jesus Johosheba and Jehoida Jeroboam Noah Nehemiah	Anne Frank Volunteer organizations Leaders throughout history	Wilderness survival Problem-solving		Practice making decisions/taking initiative/solving problems Leadership skills	Diorama Clay model	"Seek Ye First the Kingdom of God"	_Swiss Family Robinson_ _Puss and boots_ _The Wind and the Sun_ _The Borrowers_ _My Side of the Mountain_ _The Diary of Anne Frank_ Journal diary - writing Survival manual writing	Wilderness survival trip Library
FRONTIER LIFE	Col. 1 Col. 3	Westward settlement Frontier life Laura Ingalls Wilder	Bartering Herbs	Herbal medicine Log-splitting Frontier games Square-dancing	Frontier cooking Preserving/pickling Quilting bee Sewing bee One-room schoolhouse Harvest festival with neighbors or co-op	Model log cabin Soddy Candle-making Whittling Sewing clothing Soap-making Hand-sewing Rug-hooking Quilting Baseball Rag doll	Country music	Frontier life/settler books _Little House on the Prairie_ and other books by Laura Ingalls Wilder Caddie Woodlawn	Country store
WORK AND SIMPLE MACHINES	Gen. 1:26-28 Gen. 3	Archimedes Sir Isaac Newton	Work Newton's Laws of Motion Simple machines Problem-solving	Leap frog Tennis Baseball Golf Bowling Jacks Rowing Fishing Weight-lifting Rollerskating Skateboarding Bike riding	Using simple machines at home	Mobile Carving Lineoleum-block printing Pinewood or Soapbox Derby car Windlass Woodworking project Junk art	Work songs "Drill, Ye Terriers, Drill" "I've Been Workin' on the Railroad" "Volga Boat Song" "Erie Canal" "Just Whistle While You Work"	Books about work and simple machines Biography of Isaac Newton	Machine shop Assembly line Transmission shop/auto parts store Elevator Crane Sports store Local dump
ENERGY	Col. 1:16, 17 Holy Spirit	Energy Sources and uses through history	Energy (muscular, chemical, nuclear, electrical, heat, light, steam, solar, sonar, wind, water, mechanical)	Pea shooters	Using energy at home	"Land Sailor" craft Kite Splatter painting Solar print Wood-burning Pinwheel	_William Tell Overture_ _Moonlight Sonata_	Books about energy and power	Dry cleaners
ELECTRICAL/ MAGNETISM	Col. 1:16, 17	Benjamin Franklin Luigi Galvani Alessandro Volta Hans Christian Oersted Andre Marie Ampere Michael Faraday George Simon Ohm Samuel Morse Alexander Graham Bell Guglielmo Marconi Thomas Edison	Electricity Magnetism Electromagnetism	Electrical safety	Family electrical repairs Estimating and conserving electrical use	Electroquiz game Busy box Magnet-writer Magnet Masterpiece Motor Morse code transmitter Lightbulb Motion picture "camera"	"Bunny Hop" "Virginia Reel" "I've Been Workin' on the Railroad" "Little Red Caboose" "Drill, Ye Terriers, Drill" Beach Boys' car songs	Electricity and magnetism books Biographies of Franklin, Edison, and Faraday "Radio broadcasting"	Hardware or lighting store Electrician Transformer Generator Dam

KONOS OVERVIEW · VOLUME III

	BIBLE	SOCIAL STUDIES	SCIENCE/MATH	HEALTH/P.E.	PRACTICAL LIVING	ARTS/CRAFTS	MUSIC	LANGUAGE/ LITERATURE	FIELD TRIPS
INDUSTRIAL REVOLUTION/ INVENTIONS	Col. 3:23 Eph. 4:28 II Thess. 3:10 Lk. 19:13	Famous inventors and industrialists Industrial Revolution	Famous inventions Trains Cars Horsepower	Unsanitary working conditions Tug of War Paddle boating	Home gadgets "Pre-plow" gardening Shoveling "coal" Home "assembly" line Car repairs Inventive family games	Steam engine Model paddle boat Drawing cars Go-cart Model cars Your own invention(s)		Books about inventions Books about trains and cars Biographies of famous inventors *Mike Mulligan and the Steam Shovel* Reading and writing	Farm equipment store Steam locomotive Lawn mower shop Oil refinery Car assembly plant Car mechanic

	BIBLE	SOCIAL STUDIES	SCIENCE/MATH	HEALTH/P.E.	PRACTICAL LIVING	ARTS/CRAFTS	MUSIC	LANGUAGE/ LITERATURE	FIELD TRIPS
JOY/ CHEERFULNESS		Cheerful people Comedians Clowns		Acrobatics					

DOES KONOS MEET STATE REQUIREMENTS?

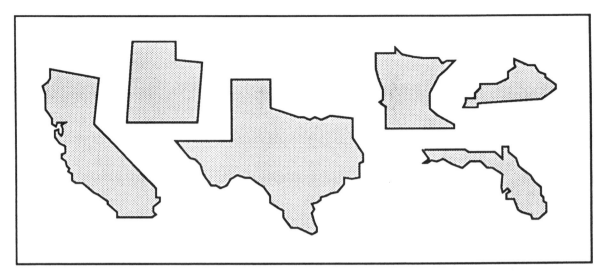

Although KONOS CURRICULUM was not formulated in order to meet state requirements, by fully equipping our children in what we believe the Lord wants for our children, we find that we do, in fact, provide all that is required by the state *and much more!* KONOS includes all that is required by the state, but has not stopped there. KONOS children are also exposed to Bible, Christian values, biographies of Christians, and practice in character development. In addition, they learn practical living skills, such as:

- choosing friends
- meal planning
- budgeting and tithing money
- shopping and using catalogs
- maintaining a safe home
- handling emotions
- electrical repairs

- child care
- scheduling time
- manners
- loving the unlovable
- helping the handicapped
- decision making
- sewing

On the following pages is a comparison of what the state requires and what KONOS provides. The regular type indicates what the state requires; the bold type is what KONOS provides. You will see that, within three volumes, KONOS covers what is normally taught. In other words, the *scope* is the same (although KONOS covers more), while the *sequence* may be different. The sequence or the order in which certain subjects are taught is very arbitrary. Except for subjects (like math and language) which build upon previously learned skills, there is no necessary order for learning topics. For example, what does it matter if the topic of birds is learned before or after the topic of beavers? In fact, even within the state requirements, there is a diversity about *when* to teach the topics (as noted by superscripts). If, for some reason, you want to follow the state's guidelines for what is taught at each level, you can use all three KONOS volumes during the year. However, we do not recommend spending money when it is unnecessary.

STATE SCOPE & SEQUENCE* AND **KONOS****

GRADE K

Science

Plant life[K-3]
I: Patience - Plant Growth/Gardening

Animal life[K-3]
I: Patience - Animal Birth/Growth
I: Orderliness - Animal Classification

**History/
Social Studies**

Myself and others
I: Honor - Heredity/Individuality
III: Cooperation

Art/Drama

Sensory awareness[K-1]
I: Attentiveness - Ears/Sound Music
I: Attentiveness - Eyes/Seeing
I: Attentiveness - Other Senses

Music

Listening[K-3]
I: Attentiveness - Ears/Sound/Music

Body movement[K-3]
III: Self-control - Dance

Playing percussion instruments[K-1]
I: Attentiveness - Ears/Sound/Music

Literature

Nursery rhymes[K-1]
Many other units

Short poems[K-1]
III: Self-control - Poetry
Many other units

Animal Stories[K-1]
I: Orderliness - Animal Classification
I: Attentiveness - Birds
I: Obedience - Horses
I: Trust - Sheep
II: Responsibility - Beavers
II: Responsibility - Ants
II: Responsibility - Pet Care
III: Cooperation - Bees
III: Determination - Expeditions (Ocean Life)
Many other units

Health/Safety

Rest and sleep[K-1]
I: Stewardship of the Body - Rest

Hearing and vision care[K-1]
I: Attentiveness - Ears/Sound/Music
I: Attentiveness - Eyes/Seeing

Food groups[K-1]
I: Stewardship of the Body - Nutrition

Emotions[K-1]
III: Self-control - Emotions

Friends[K-1]
II: Wisdom - General (Choosing Friends)
II: Love/Generosity - General (Loving others)
II: Loyalty - General (Being a good friend)

Dental care[K-1]
I: Stewardship of the Body - Abuse/ Prevention
III: Cooperation - Systems of the Body

Physical Education

Marching, skipping, galloping, ball throwing ball kicking, small apparatus, jumping rope[K-1]
I: Stewardship of the Body - Exercise
Many other units

GRADE 1

Science

Plant parts and functions[K-3]
- I: **Orderliness - Plant Classification**
- I: **Patience - Plant Growth/Gardening**

Animal characteristics and classification[K-3]
- I: **Orderliness - Animal Classification**
- I: **Attentiveness - Birds**
- I: **Obedience - Horses**
- I: **Trust - Sheep**
- II: **Responsibility - Beavers**

- II: **Responsibility - Ants**
- III: **Cooperation - Bees**
- III: **Determination - Expeditions (Ocean Life)**

Planets/Moons[K-3]
- I: **Orderliness - Solar System**

Night/Day[K-3]
- I: **Orderliness - Calendars/Seasons**

**History/
Social Studies**

People at home and at school
- III: **Cooperation - Family/Church**
- **Most other units**

Art/Drama

Sensory awareness[K-3]
- I: **Attentiveness - Ears/Sound/Music**
- I: **Attentiveness - Eyes/Seeing**
- I: **Attentiveness - Other senses**

Music

Listening[K-3]
- I: **Attentiveness - Ears/Sound/Music**

Body movement[K-3]
- III: **Self-control - Body Movement/Dance**

Playing percussion instruments[K-3]
- I: **Attentiveness - Ears/Sound/Music**

Literature

Nursery rhymes[K-1]
- **Many units**

Short poems[K-1]
- III: **Self-control - Poetry**
- **Most other units**

Folk and fairy tales[K-1]
- I: **Honor/Respect - Countries/Cultures**
- **Many other units**

Health/Safety

Doctors, dentists, disease[K-1]
- I: **Stewardship of the Body - Abuse/
  Prevention**

Cooperation in the family[K-1]
- III: **Cooperation - Family/Church**
- **Most other units**

**Physical
Education**

Marching, skipping, galloping, ball throwing
ball kicking, small apparatus, jumping rope[K-1]
- I: **Stewardship of the Body - Exercise**
- **Many other units**

STATE SCOPE & SEQUENCE* AND KONOS**

GRADE 2

Science

Human Senses[K-3]
I: **Attentiveness - Ears/Sound/Music**
I: **Attentiveness - Eyes/Seeing**
I: **Attentiveness - Other senses**

Human Growth[K-3]
I: **Patience - Human Birth/Growth**

Stars[K-3]
II: **Inquisitiveness - Explorers/Navigation/Sailing**

Rocks[K-3]
I: **Orderliness - Rock Classification**

Soil[K-3]
I: **Stewardship of Natural Resources**

Air[K-3]
I: **Trust - Flight and Airplanes**

Wind[K-3]
II: **Inquisitiveness - Weather**

Sound[K-3]
I: **Attentiveness - Ears/Sound/Music**

History/Social Studies

People as members of groups
I: **Honor/Respect - Countries/Cultures and Kindness/Service/Etiquette**

II: **Inquisitiveness - The Earth**
III: **Cooperation - Family/Church**
Other units

Art/Drama

Variety of media
All units

Music

Listening[K-3]
I: **Attentiveness - Ears/Sound/Music**

Body movements[K-3]
III: **Self-control - Dance**

Pantomime
III: **Self-control - Dance**

Literature

Fables[2-3]
Several units

People stories[2-3]
Most units
I: **Honor/Respect - Heredity/Individuality and Countries/Cultures**

Health/Safety

Handicaps[2-3]
III: **Determination - Handicaps**

Exercise
I: **Stewardship of the Body - Exercise**
III: **Cooperation - Systems of the Body (Muscular)**

Nutrition
I: **Stewardship of the Body - Nutrition**

Disease
I: **Stewardship of the Body - Abuse/Prevention**

III: **Cooperation - Systems of the Body (Immune)**

Animal parenting/Infant care
I: **Patience - Animal Birth/Growth**
I: **Patience - Human Birth/Growth**

Multi-ethnic groups
I: **Honor/Respect - Heredity/Individuality**
III: **Cooperation - States and Regions**

Media Influences
III: **Honesty - Newspapers**
III: **Honesty - Business and Advertising**

Physical Education

Balance, tumbling, muscle building[2-3]
I: **Stewardship of the Body - Exercise**
III: **Cooperation - Systems of the Body (Muscular)**

Folk dance[2-3]
I: **Honor/Respect - Countries/Cultures**
III: **Self-control - Dance**

STATE SCOPE & SEQUENCE* AND **KONOS****

GRADE 3

Science

Machines^{K-3}
III: **Initiative/Resourcefulness - Work and
Simple Machines**

Friction^{K-3}
I: **Obedience - Friction and Resistance**

Motion^{K-3}
I: **Obedience - Action-Reaction**

Oceans^{K-3}
II: **Inquisitiveness - The Earth**
III: **Determination - Expeditions (Sea)**

Matter^{K-3}
III: **Determination - Atomic Research**

Shadows^{K-3}
II: **Inquisitiveness - Scientists/Scientific
Method**

Electricity and Magnets^{K-3}
III: **Initiative/Resourcefulness - Electricity/
Magnetism**

Sound^{K-3}
I: **Attentiveness - Ears/Sound/Music**

**History/
Social Studies**

People as members of communities
III: **Cooperation - Town/Community and
Family/Church**

Art/Drama

Art/Drama
Oral communication
Most units
III: **Self-control - Speech**

Music

Listening^{K-3}
I: **Attentiveness - Ears/Sound/Music**

Body Movement^{K-3}
III: **Self-control - Body/Appetites and
Dance**

Literature

Puppet shows$^{2-3}$
Several units
III: **Self-control - Speech**

Humor$^{2-3}$
Many units
I: **Stewardship of the Body - Fun**
III: **Self-control - Poetry**

Health/Safety

Disabilities
III: **Determination - Handicaps**

Digestion
III: **Cooperation - Systems of the Body
(Digestive)**

Individuality
I: **Honor/Respect - Heredity/Individuality**

Family unit
Most units
III: **Cooperation - Family/Church**

**Physical
Education**

Tumbling and games
I: **Stewardship of the Body - Exercise**

Ethnic dance
I: **Honor/Respect - Countries and Cultures**
III: **Cooperation - State and Regions**
III: **Self-control - Dance**

STATE SCOPE & SEQUENCE* AND **KONOS****

GRADE 4

Science	Cells[3-6] **III: Cooperation – Systems of the Body** Plant life[3-6] **I: Patience - Plant Growth/Gardening** Fungi[3-6] **I: Patience - Grain/Bread/Yeast** Ecosystems[3-6] **I: Attentiveness - Predator and Prey** **I: Stewardship of Natural Resources** Seasons[3-6] **I: Orderliness - Calendars/Seasons** Temperatures[3-6] **I: Orderliness - Counting/Measuring** **II: Inquisitiveness - Weather**	Light[3-6] **I: Obedience - Light/Authority** **II: Inquisitiveness - Scientists/Scientific Method** Solar system **I: Orderliness - Solar System** **II: Inquisitiveness - Explorers/Navigation/ Sailing (Constellations)** Rock and mineral classification[3-6] **I: Orderliness - Rock Classification** Weathering[3-6] **I: Stewardship of Natural Resources** Geologic features[3-6] **II: Inquisitiveness - The Earth**
History/ Social Studies	State history **III: Cooperation - States and Regions**	
Art/Drama	Improvisation/Drama **Most units**	
Music	Music theory[4-6] **KONOS COLLAGE (to be published)** Identifying instruments[4-6] **I: Attentiveness - Ears/Sound/Music**	Singing[4-6] **III: Self-control - Singing** Dancing[4-6] **III: Self-control - Dance**
Literature	Myth/Legend[4-6] **III: Honesty - Books** Historical chronicles and fiction[4-6] **Each unit in Volume II (American History)** **Many other units**	Biographies[4-6] **Most units** Newspaper articles[4-6] **III: Honesty - Newspapers** Children's magazines[4-6] **III: Honesty - Newspapers and other media**
Health/Safety	Nutrition **I: Stewardship of the Body - Nutrition** Growth and Heredity **I: Patience - Human Birth/Growth** **I: Honor - Heredity/Individuality**	Safety **II: Wisdom - Safety**
Physical Education	Games **Many units**	Creative dance **III: Self-control - Dance**

STATE SCOPE & SEQUENCE* AND **KONOS****

GRADE 5

Science

Animal classification[3-6]
I: Orderliness - Animal Classification

Animal reproduction and growth [3-6]
I: Patience - Animal Birth/Growth

Pet care[3-6]
II: Responsibility - Pet Care

Air pressure[3-6]
I: Trust - Flight and Airplanes
II: Inquisitiveness - Weather

Chemical symbols[3-6]
III: Determination - Atomic Research

Force/Friction[3-6]
I: Obedience - Friction and Resistance

Simple machines[3-6]
III: Initiative/Resourcefulness - Work and Simple Machines

Energy[3-6]
III: Initiative/Resourcefulness - Energy

Conservation of energy[3-6]
I: Stewardship of Natural Resources

History/ Social Studies

People of a nation
II: Inquisitiveness - Explorers
II: Responsibility - Early Settlers
II: Courage - Revolutionary War
II: Wisdom - Government
II: Loyalty - Citizenship

I: Attentiveness - Frontiersmen/Tracking/ Trapping
III: Resourcefulness - Frontier Life
III: Cooperation - States and Regions (Civil War)
III: Resourcefulness - Industrial Revolution

Art/Drama

Dramatic presentations
II: Responsibility - Early Settlers (Thanksgiving Tabloid)
II: Generosity - Christmas (Christmas Play)

II: Loyalty - Citizenship (The Birth of America One-man Show)
III: Cooperation - States and Regions (A Walk Through America)

Music

Identifying instruments[4-6]
I: Attentiveness - Ears/Sound/Music

Singing[4-6]
III: Self-Control - Singing

Dancing[4-6]
III: Self-control - Dance

Literature

Advertising[4-6]
III: Honesty - Business and Advertising

Mystery/Detective fiction[4-6]
II: Inquisitiveness - Detectives

Adventure tales[4-6]
Several units
III: Determination - Expeditions

Health/Safety

Skeletal and muscular systems
III: Cooperation - Systems of the Body (Skeletal and Muscular)

Nutrition
I: Stewardship of the Body - Nutrition

Genetic traits
I: Honor/Respect - Heredity/Individuality

First aid
II: Wisdom - Safety

Physical Education

Aerobics
I: Stewardship of the Body - Exercise
III: Cooperation - Systems of the Body (Muscular)

Gymnastics
III: Determination - Olympics and Physical Skills

Basketball

Square dance
III: Initiative/Resourcefulness - Frontier Life

STATE SCOPE & SEQUENCE* AND **KONOS****

GRADE 6

Science

Human anatomy[3-6]
III: Cooperation - Systems of the Body

Human reproduction and growth[3-6]
I: Patience - Human Birth/Growth

Light/Color[3-6]
I: Obedience - Authority/Light
II: Inquisitiveness - Scientists/Scientific
Method

Optics[3-6]
I: Trust - Deception/Illusion

Magnets/Electricity[3-6]
III: Initiative/Resourcefulness - Electricity/
Magnetism

Compass[3-6]
II: Inquisitiveness - Explorers/Navigation/
Sailing

Sound[3-6]
I: Attentiveness - Ears/Sound/Music

History/
Social Studies

Our world, its diverse people and their
societies
I: Honor/Respect - Countries/Cultures
II: Inquisitiveness - The Earth

Art/Drama

Playwriting[6-7]
Several units

Music

Identifying instruments[4-6]
I: Attentiveness - Ears/Sound/Music

Singing[4-6]
III: Self-Control - Singing

Dancing[4-6]
III: Self-control - Dance

Literature

Narrative poetry[4-6]
Many units
III: Self-control - Poetry

Tall tales and puns[4-6]
I: Attentiveness - Frontiersmen/Track-
ing/Trapping
III: Honesty - Books

Proverbs[4-6]
Many units
III: Self-control - Speech

Health/Safety

Physical activities
I: Stewardship of the Body - Exercise
III: Cooperation - Systems of the Body
(Muscular)
III: Determination - Olympics and Physi-
cal Skills
Other units

Nutrition
I: Stewardship of the Body - Nutrition

Parental Values
Every unit

STATE SCOPE & SEQUENCE* AND KONOS**

GRADE 7

Science

Energy[6-9]
III: Resourcefulness - Energy

Heredity/Genetics[6-9]
I: Honor/Respect - Heredity/Individuality

Creation/Evolution[6-9]
I: Orderliness - The Creation

Plant growth and metabolism[6-9]
I: Patience - Plant Growth/Gardening

Protozoa, bacteria, virus[6-9]
III: Cooperation - Systems of the Body (Immune)

Animal reproduction and development[6-9]
I: Patience - Animal Birth/Growth

Seasons[6-9]
I: Orderliness - Calendars/Seasons

Geology[6-9]
II: Inquisitiveness - The Earth

Oceanography[6-9]
III: Determination - Expeditions (Sea)

Atoms/Molecules/Compounds[6-9]
III: Determination - Atomic Research

Radioactivity/Fission/Fusion[6-9]
III: Determination - Atomic Research

Complex machines[6-9]
III: Initiative/Resourcefulness - Industrial Revolution/Inventions

Work/Power/Energy[6-9]
III: Initiative/Resourcefulness - Work and Simple Machines and Energy

Electric current[6-9]
III: Initiative/Resourcefulness - Electricity/ Magnetism

Sound[6-9]
I: Attentiveness - Ears/Sound/Music

History/ Social Studies

The Changing World
II: Wisdom - Government (Current affairs)

Art/Drama

Playwriting
Several units

Variety of media
I: Orderliness - Creating

Music

Ethnic music
I: Honor/Respect - Countries/Cultures
II: Inquisitiveness - The Earth

Dance
III: Self-control - Dance

Instrument - playing
I: Attentiveness - Ears/Sound/Music

Literature

Short stories
Most Units

Journals, diaries, letters
Several units in Volume II
Many other units.

Lyric and narrative poems
III: Self-control - Poetry
Other Units

Novels
Most Units

Weekly news magazines
III: Honesty - Newspapers and Other Media

Historical documents
Many units in Volume II (American History)

GRADE 7

Health/Safety	Heart, lung, circulatory disorders **III: Cooperation - Systems of the Body**	Reproductive process **I: Patience - Human Birth/Growth** **III: Self-control - Body/Appetites**
Physical Education	Rhythm and dance **III: Self-control - Dance** Conditioning **I: Stewardship of the Body - Exercise** **III: Cooperation Systems of the Body** **(Muscular)**	Sports and gymnastics **III: Determination - Olympics and Physical** **Skills**

STATE SCOPE & SEQUENCE* AND KONOS**

GRADE 8

Science

Energy
III: Initiative/Resourcefulness - Energy

Heredity-Genetics
I: Honor/Respect - Heredity/Individuality

Creation/Evolution
I: Orderliness - Creating

Plant growth/metabolism
I: Patience - Plant Growth/Gardening

Protozoa, bacteria, virus
III: Cooperation - Systems of the Body (Immune)

Animal reproduction
I: Patience - Animal Birth/Growth

History/ Social Studies

American history and geography
II: All units
III: Cooperation - States and Regions

Art/Drama

Variety of media
I: Orderliness - Creating

Music

Four-part singing
III: Self-control - Singing

Ethnic music
I: Honor/Respect - Countries/Cultures
II: Inquisitiveness - The Earth

Dance
III: Self-control - Dance

Instrument playing
I: Attentiveness - Ears/Sound/Music

Literature

Short stories
Most Units

Poems
Most Units
III: Self-control - Poetry

Newspapers
III: Honesty - Newspapers and Other Media

Health/Safety

Exercise
I: Stewardship of the Body - Exercise
III: Cooperation - Systems of the Body (Muscular)

Human life cycle
I: Patience - Human Birth/Growth

Home safety
II: Wisdom - Safety

Physical Education

Rhythm and dance
III: Self-control - Dance

Conditioning
I: Stewardship of the Body - Exercise
III: Cooperation - Systems of the Body (Muscular)

Sports and gymnastics
III: Determination - Olympics and Physical Skills

STATE SCOPE & SEQUENCE* AND **KONOS****

HIGH SCHOOL****

Science

Biology
I: Orderliness - Animal Classification
III: Cooperation - Systems of the Body
I: Stewardship of Natural Resources

Chemistry
III: Determination - Atomic Research

Physics
I: Obedience - Friction and Resistance
III: Initiative/Resourcefulness - Work and Simple Machines, Energy, Electricity/ Magnetism, and Industrial Revolution/ Inventions

Consumer Ed/ Economics

Family
III: Cooperation - Church/Family

Financial Management
I: Stewardship of Money and Posses- sions

Food and clothing
I: Stewardship of the Body - Nutrition
I: Stewardship of Money and Posses- sions

History/ Social Studies

Citizenship and Civics
II: Inquisitiveness - The Earth
I: Honor/Respect - Countries/Cultures

World History
KONOS History of the World (to be published, Lord willing!)

The U.S.
II: All units (Early American History, Gov- ernment, Citizenship)
III: Initiative/Resourcefulness - Frontier Life
I: Attentiveness - Frontiersmen (West- ward Expansion)
III: Cooperation - States and Regions (Civil War)

Art/Drama

Plays
(See Grade 5)

Music

Chorus
III: Self-Control - Singing

Instrument playing
I: Attentiveness - Ears/Sound/Music

Literature

American Literature
Samples in Volume II and many other units

World and classical literature
Samples in
I: Honor/Respect - Countries/Cultures,
II: Inquisitiveness - The Earth
Many other units

Health/Safety

Visual and hearing disorders
I: Attentiveness - Ears/Sound/Music and Eyes/Seeing

Cardiovascular disease
III: Cooperation - Systems of the Body (Circulatory)

Human sexuality, genetic disorders
I: Patience - Human Birth/Growth
I: Stewardship of the Body - Abuse/ Prevention
III: Self-control - Body/Appetites
III Determination - Handicaps

Marriage/Parenting
III: Cooperation - Church/Family

Physical Education

Fitness
I: Stewardship of the Body - Exercise
III: Cooperation - Systems of the Body (Muscular)

Sports and gymnastics
III: Determination - Olympics and Physical Skills

Dance
III: Self-control - Dance

HIGH SCHOOL****

Industrial Education

Automotive
III: Initiative/Resourcefulness - Inventions (car engine)

Drafting

Electronics

Graphic arts

Metals

Photography

Wood

**See
I: Orderliness - Creating for all of above**

Foreign Language

Math

Algebra I, II
Geometry
Trigonomentry
Calculus

English Composition

Composition
**Writing Activities in every unit
(See KONOS COMPASS - HOW DO I
TEACH WRITING SKILLS?)**

*   State of California
** KONOS Volumes revised 1989
*** See KONOS Math and Language Checklist
**** A foundation of learning; add supplements for high-school level

HOW DOES KONOS COMPARE WITH A TYPICAL COURSE OF STUDY USED BY TEXTBOOK PUBLISHERS?

As discussed in the comparison with state requirements, the scope of what KONOS covers is the same, while the sequence may be different. On the following pages you will see an averaging of what and when topics are covered in school textbooks. You will see that KONOS does indeed cover all topics that are published by traditional textbook publishers *plus much more!* The regular print indicates what most textbook publishers require; the bold print is what KONOS provides.

Not only will your children learn better, they will also be exposed to character and practical living skills that are found in no traditional curricula. They learn good manners, how to choose friends, how to control their emotions, how to cooperate together as a family, how to be a responsible worker, how to treat handicapped people compassionately, etc., etc. while not sacrificing anything academically. In fact, by teaching the KONOS way, children learn and retain much more.

11

TYPICAL COURSE OF STUDY* AND **KONOS****

GRADE K

Social Studies

Meaning of holidays
I: Orderliness - Calendars/Seasons

Role of home and family
All units
III: Cooperation - Family/Church

Characteristics of home and family
All units
III: Cooperation - Family/Church

Location and diagram of home and school
II: Inquisitiveness - The Earth

Relationship between home and school

Relationship of individual to the group
III: Cooperation - Family/Church

Children in other lands
I: Honor/Respect - Countries/Culture

Why and how things change
I: Patience - Plant Birth and Growth

Where things come from
I: Orderliness - Creating

What people do (jobs)
I: Stewardship of Talents - Careers
Many other units

Science

Weather and seasons (observations)
II: Inquisitiveness - Weather

Interrelationships of plants and animals
I: Stewardship of Natural Resources

The sun–our principal source of energy
II: Inquisitiveness - Scientists/Scientific Method
I: Orderliness - Solar System

Classification of living things
I: Orderliness - Plant Classification
I: Orderliness - Animal Classification

Simple measurements
I: Orderliness - Counting/Measuring

How plants are alike and different
I: Orderliness - Plant Classification

Farm animals
I: Orderliness - Animal Classification
II: Responsibility - Pet Care

Observing animals
I: Orderliness - Animal Classification
I: Patience - Animal Birth and Growth

Indoor plants
I: Patience - Plant Birth and Growth

Earth, moon, and stars
I: Orderliness - Solar System
II: Inquisitiveness - The Earth

Health and Safety

Personal hygiene
I: Stewardship of the Body - Abuse/Prevention

Good Eating Habits
I: Stewardship of the Body - Nutrition

Good clothing habits
I: Orderliness - Regularity/Discipline

Care of teeth
I: Stewardship of the Body - Abuse/Prevention

Safety to and from school
II: Wisdom - Safety

Language Arts***

Arithmetic***

TYPICAL COURSE OF STUDY* AND **KONOS****

GRADE 1

Social Studies

Citizenship
II: Loyalty - Citizenship

Neighborhood helpers
III: Cooperation - Town/Community

What people do (jobs)
I: Stewardship of Money and Possessions

Our American heritage
II: Early American History

National heroes
II: Early American History

School-community
III: Cooperation - Town/Community

Homes in other lands
I: Honor/Respect - Countries/Cultures

Farm and zoo
I: Orderliness - Animal Classification

Make and read a simple neighborhood map
III: Cooperation - Town/Commmunity

Holidays
I: Orderliness - Calendars/Seasons
II: Love/Generosity - Christmas and Easter
II: Responsibility - Early Settlers (Thanksgiving)

Science

Animals and pets
I: Orderliness - Animal Classification
II: Responsibility - Pet Care

Where plants live
I: Orderliness - Plant Classification

Where animals live
I: Orderliness - Animal Classification

Grouping and classification
I: Orderliness - Animal Classification
I: Orderliness - Plant Classification

Air and water
I: Trust - Flight and Airplanes
I: Trust - Floating and Ships
II: Inquisitiveness - Weather

Seeds, bulbs, plants, and flowers
I: Patience - Plant Birth and Growth
I: Orderliness - Plant Classification

Day and night
I: Orderliness - Calendars/Seasons

Sun, moon, stars
I: Orderliness - Solar System

Seasons and weather
II: Inquisitiveness - Weather
I: Orderliness - Calendars/Seasons

Fire and temperature
II: Inquisitiveness - Weather
I: Orderliness - Counting/Measuring

Simple machines
III: Resourcefulness - Simple Machines

Health and Safety

Safety rules to and from school
II: Wisdom - Safety

Good eating habits
I: Stewardship of the Body - Nutrition

How to dress for weather and activity
II: Inquisitiveness - Weather
I: Orderliness - Calendars/Seasons

Exercise and rest
I: Stewardship of the Body - Exercise
I: Stewardship of the Body - Rest

Personal hygiene
I: Stewardship of the Body - Abuse/Prevention

Language Arts***

Arithmetic***

TYPICAL COURSE OF STUDY* AND KONOS**

GRADE 2

Social Studies

Community services and helpers
III: Cooperation - Town/Community

Holidays and festivals
I: Orderliness - Calendars/Seasons
II: Love/Generosity - Christmas and Easter

Patriotic celebrations
II: Loyalty - Citizenship

Our food
I: Stewardship of the Body - Nutrition

Shelter
III: Cooperation - Town/Community

What people do (jobs)
I: Stewardship of Talents - Careers

Families and Communities in other lands
I: Honor/Respect - Countries/Cultures

World heroes
Most units in Volume II
I: Obedience - Military

Interdependence of people
III: Cooperation - Town/Community and Family/Church

Science

Animals of our neighborhood
I: Attentiveness - Predator/Prey
II: Responsibility - Pet Care

Useful and harmful animals
I: Orderliness - Classification of Animals

Birds and insects in winter
I: Orderliness - Calendars/Seasons

Animal babies
I: Patience - Animal Birth and Growth

How plants and animals get their food
I: Patience - Plant Birth and Growth
I: Patience - Animal Birth and Growth

Plant reproduction
I: Patience - Plant Birth and Growth

How animals protect themselves
I: Attentiveness - Predator/Prey

Effects of seasons
I: Orderliness - Calendars/Seasons

Weather
II: Inquisitiveness - Weather

Heat and temperature
II: Inquisitiveness - Weather

The sun
I: Orderliness - Solar System
II: Inquisitiveness - Weather

The moon
I: Orderliness - Solar System

The earth and sky
I: Orderliness - Solar System

Simple Constellations
II: Inquisitiveness - Explorers/Navigation/Sailing

Gravity
I: Orderliness - Solar System

Air and atmosphere
II: Inquisitiveness - The Earth and Weather

Magnets and forces
III: Resourcefulness - Electricity/Magnetism

Exploring space
I: Trust - Flight and Airplanes

Health and Safety

Know basic food groups
I: Stewardship of the Body - Nutrition

Dental hygiene
I: Stewardship of the Body - Abuse/Prevention

Personal cleanliness
I: Stewardship of the Body - Abuse/Prevention

Safety in the neighborhood
I: Trust - Deception/Illusion
II: Wisdom - Safety

Communicable diseases
III: Cooperation - Systems of the Body (Immune)

Preventive measures against disease
I: Stewardship of the Body - Abuse/Prevention

Language Arts***
Arithmetic***

TYPICAL COURSE OF STUDY* AND **KONOS****

GRADE 3

Social Studies

Community helpers
III: Cooperation - Town/Community

Kinds of careers
I: Stewardship of Talents - Careers

History and development of local community
III: Cooperation - Town/Community

American Indians and pioneers
I: Attentiveness - Indians
I: Attentiveness - Frontiersmen
III: Initiative/Resourcefulness - Frontier Life

Shelters of animals and people
I: Orderliness - Animal Classification
III: Cooperation - Town/Community

Transportation today and yesterday
I: Trust - Flight/Airplanes and Floating/Ships
III: Resourcefulness - Industrial Revolution/Inventions

Communication today and yesterday
I: Attentiveness - Ears/Sound/Music
III: Resourcefulness - Industrial Revolution/Inventions

Sources of our food
I: Stewardship of the Body - Nutrition
I: Patience - Plant Growth/Gardening

Sources of our clothing
I: Trust - Shepherd/Sheep/Weaving
III: Resourcefulness - Industrial Revolution/Inventions

Shelter
III: Cooperation - Town/Community

Some great Americans
Many units especially in Volume II

Holidays and folk customs
I: Orderliness - Calendars/Seasons
II: Love/Generosity - Christmas and Easter

Flat maps and the globe
II: Inquisitiveness - The Earth

Science

How the face of the earth is changed
II: Inquisitiveness - The Earth

The atmosphere
II: Inquisitiveness - Weather

Motions of the earth
I: Orderliness - Solar System and Calendars/Seasons

Earth satellites
I: Trust - Flight/Airplanes

Stars and moon
II: Inquisitiveness - Explorers/Navigation/Sailing
I: Orderliness - Solar System

Energy and its sources
III: Resourcefulness - Energy

Sound
I: Attentiveness - Ears/Sound/Music

Weather and climate
II: Inquisitiveness - Weather

Rocks and soil
I: Orderliness - Rock Classification
II: Inquisitiveness - The Earth

How animals serve people
I: Orderliness - Animal Classification

Plants and animals of the desert
III: Cooperation - States/Regions

Plants and animals of the sea
III: Determination - Expeditions (Underwater)

Life cycle of animals
I: Patience - Animal Birth and Growth

Common birds, trees, and flowers
I: Attentiveness - Birds
I: Orderliness - Plant Classification

Forest plants
I: Orderliness - Plant Classification

Conservation of plants and animals
I: Stewardship of Natural Resources

Ocean life
I: Orderliness - Animal Classification
III: Determination - Expeditions

Magnets and electricity
III: Resourcefulness - Electricity/Magnetism

Great names in science
II: Inquisitiveness - Scientists/Scientific Method
Other units

GRADE 3

Health and Safety

Correct names for various parts of the body
III: Cooperation - Systems of the Body

Simple first aid
II: Wisdom - Safety

Proper balance of activities
I: Orderliness - Regularity/Discipline
I: Stewardship of the Body

Prevention and control of diseases
I: Stewardship of the Body - Abuse/ Prevention
III: Cooperation - Systems of the Body (Immune)

Care of eyes and ears
I: Attentiveness - Ears/Sound/Music and Eyes/Seeing

Health with relation to food, shelter, and clothing
I: Stewardship of the Body

Safety in the community
I: Trust - Deception/Illusion
II: Wisdom - Safety
II: Cooperation - Town/Community

Language Arts***

Arithmetic***

TYPICAL COURSE OF STUDY* AND **KONOS****

GRADE 4

Social Studies	History and development of the local state **III: Cooperation - States/Regions**	Types of community life **III: Cooperation - Town/Community**
	Relationship of the state to its region, the nation, and the world **III: Cooperation - States/Regions**	Why we have laws **I: Obedience - Crime and Punishment** **II: Wisdom - Government**
	Geographic or climatic regions of the world **II: Inquisitiveness - The Earth**	The globe **II: Inquisitiveness - The Earth**

Science	Environment of local state **III: Cooperation - States/Regions**	Oceans and the hydrosphere **II: Inquisitiveness - The Earth**
	Measurement systems (including metric) **I: Orderliness - Counting/Measuring**	Climate **II: Inquisitiveness - Weather**
	Plants and animals of the past **I: Orderliness - Plant Classification and Animal Classification**	Rocks and minerals **I: Orderliness - Rock Classification** **II: Inquisitiveness - The Earth**
	Earth and its history **II: Inquisitiveness - The Earth**	Plants and seeds **I: Patience - Plant Birth and Growth**
	Balance of nature **I: Stewardship - Stewardship of Natural Resources**	The insect world **I: Orderliness - Animal Classification** **II: Responsibility - Ants** **III: Cooperation - Bees**
	Classification systems **I: Orderliness - Plant Classification and Animal Classification**	Biological organization **I: Orderliness - Plant and Animal Classification**
	Structure of plants **I: Patience - Plant Birth and Growth** **I: Orderliness - Plant Classification**	Living in space **I: Trust - Flight/Airplanes**
	Influence of weather **II: Inquisitiveness - Weather**	Air and water pollution **I: Stewardship - Stewardship of Natural Resources**
	Causes of seasons **I: Orderliness - Calendars/Seasons**	Great names in science **II: Inquisitiveness - Scientists/Scientific Method**
	Solar system and the universe **I: Orderliness - Solar System**	

Health and Safety	The body and its functions **III: Cooperation - Systems of the Body**	Principles of digestion **III: Cooperation - Systems of the Body**
	Care and proper use of the body **I: Stewardship of the Body**	Basic food groups and good nutrition habits **I: Stewardship of the Body - Nutrition**
	Personal and mental hygiene **I: Stewardship of the Body**	

TYPICAL COURSE OF STUDY* AND **KONOS****

GRADE 5

Social Studies

Exploration and discovery
II: Inquisitiveness - Explorers/Navigation/Sailing

Settlements in the New World
II: Responsibility - Early Settlers

Colonial life in America
II: Responsibility - Early Settlers

Pioneer life in America
III: Resourcefulness - Frontier Life

Westward movement
I: Attentiveness - Frontiersmen

Industrial and cultural growth
III: Resourcefulness - Industrial Revolution/Inventions

Life in the United States today
III: Cooperation - States/Regions

Presidents and other famous people
II: Wisdom - Presidents

Natural resources of the United States
III: Cooperation - States/Regions

Environmental issues
I: Stewardship - Stewardship of Natural Resources

Geography of the United States
III: Cooperation - States/Regions

Canada
II: Inquisitiveness - The Earth

Comparative cultures of Canada
II: Inquisitiveness - The Earth

Fundamental map skills
II: Inquisitiveness - The Earth

Science

How living things adapt
I: Attentiveness - Predator/Prey
I: Orderliness - Plant Classification and Animal Classification

Plants and their food
I: Patience - Plant Growth/Gardening and Bread/Grain/Yeast

Properties of air
I: Trust - Flight and Airplanes
II: Inquisitiveness - Weather

Properties of water
III: Initiative/Resourcefulness - Energy

Chemical systems
III: Determination - Atomic Research

Force
I: Obedience - Friction and Resistance

Time and seasons
I: Orderliness - Calendars/Seasons

Molds
I: Patience - Bread/Grain/Yeast

Bacteria
III: Cooperation - Systems of the Body (Immune)

Trees
I: Orderliness - Plant Classification

Sun
III: Initiative/Resourcefulness - Energy
I: Orderliness - Solar System

Milky Way
II: Inquisitiveness - Explorers/Navigational Sailing

Great names in science
II: Inquisitiveness - Scientists/Scientific Method

Uses and control of electricity
III: Initiative/Resourcefulness - Electricity/Magnetism

Magnetic fields
III: Initiative/Resourcefulness - Electricity/Magnetism

Latitude and longitude
II: Inquisitiveness - The Earth

Space and space explorations
I: Trust - Flight/Airplanes

Conservation
I: Stewardship - Stewardship of Natural Resources

Biotic communities
I: Stewardship - Stewardship of Natural Resources

Biological adaptations
I: Orderliness - Creating

TYPICAL COURSE OF STUDY* AND **KONOS****

GRADE 5

**Health
and Safety**

Elementary first aid
II: Wisdom - Safety

Community health resources
III: Cooperation - Town/Community

Our water supply
III: Cooperation - Town/Community

Sewage Disposal
III: Cooperation - Town/Community

Bicycle and water safety
II: Wisdom - Safety

Care of the eyes
I: Attentiveness - Eyes/Seeing

Dental hygiene
**I: Stewardship of the Body - Abuse/
Prevention**

Nutrition and diet
I: Stewardship of the Body - Nutrition

Facts about coffee, tea, soft drinks, candy,
etc.
I: Stewardship of the Body - Nutrition

Germ-bearing insects and pests
**III: Cooperation - Systems of the Body
(Immune)**

**Language
Arts*****

Arithmetic***

TYPICAL COURSE OF STUDY* AND **KONOS****

GRADE 6

Social Studies

World Cultures
II: Inquisitiveness - The Earth

Science

Helpful and harmful insects
I: Orderliness - Animal Classification

Classification of living things
I: Orderliness - Plant Classification and Animal Classification

Food for growth and energy
I: Stewardship of the Body - Nutrition

Microbes
III: Cooperation - Systems of the Body

Algae and fungi
I: Patience - Grain/Bread/Yeast

Energy and simple machines
III: Initiative/Resourcefulness - Energy and Simple Machines

Climate and weather
II: Inquisitiveness - Weather

Motors and engines
III: Initiative/Resourcefulness - Industrial Revolution/Inventions

Electricity and its uses
III: Initiative/Resourcefulness - Electricity and Magnetism

Simple astronomy
I: Orderliness - Solar System

Elementary geology
II: Inquisitiveness - The Earth

Elements of sound
I: Attentiveness - Ears/Sound/Music

Light and heat
I: Obedience - Authority/Light

Heat Engines
III: Initiative/Resourcefulness - Industrial Revolution/Inventions

Atom and nuclear energy
III: Determination - Atomic Research

Inventions and discoveries
III: Initiative/Resourcefulness - Industrial Revolution/Inventions

Great names in science
III: Initiative/Resourcefulness - Industrial Revolution/Inventions
II: Inquisitiveness - Scientists/Scientific Method

Space and space travel
I: Trust - Flight and Airplanes

Ecology, environment, and conservation
I: Stewardship of Natural Resources

Health and Safety

Cure and prevention of common diseases
I: Stewardship of the Body - Abuse/Prevention

Facts on tobacco, alcohol, and narcotics
I: Stewardship of the Body - Abuse/Prevention

Great names in the field of health
III: Cooperation - Systems of the Body

Foods
I: Stewardship of the Body - Nutrition

The heart
III: Cooperation - Systems of the Body

Safety and first aid
II: Wisdom - Safety

Personal appearance
I: Orderliness - Regularity/Discipline

Health maintenance
I: Stewardship of the Body

TYPICAL COURSE OF STUDY* AND **KONOS****

GRADE 7

Social Studies

Europe
II: Inquisitiveness - The Earth

Africa
II: Inquisitiveness - The Earth

Eastern Hemisphere
II: Inquisitiveness - The Earth

Greece, Rome
KONOS History of the World (to be published, Lord willing!)

Middle Ages
I: Obedience - Kings and Queens

Age of Discovery
II: Inquisitiveness - Explorers/Navigation/ Sailing

Industrial Age
III: Initiative/Resourcefulness - Industrial Revolution/Inventions

The family
III: Cooperation - Church/Family

Exploring careers
I: Stewardship of Talents - Careers
Many other units

Science

Scientific method
II: Inquisitiveness - Scientists and Scientific Method

The cell
III: Cooperation - Systems of the Body

Life cycle of insects
I: Orderliness - Classification of Animals

Anatomy and physiology
III: Cooperation - Systems of the Body

Genetics
I: Honor/Respect - Heredity/Individuality

Rocks, soil and minerals
I: Orderliness - Rock Classification
II: Inquisitiveness - The Earth

Air Pressure
I: Trust - Flight and Airplanes

Atmosphere
II: Inquisitiveness - Weather

Energy sources
III: Initiative/Resourcefulness - Energy

Conservation
I: Stewardship of Natural Resources
II: Inquisitiveness - Weather

Ecology and environment
I: Stewardship of Natural Resources
II: Inquisitiveness - Weather

Famous Scientists and their contributions
II: Inquisitiveness - Scientists/Scientific Method

Health and Safety

Health habits
I: Stewardship of the Body - Abuse/ Prevention

Personal and public safety
II: Wisdom - Safety

Circulation and respiration
III: Cooperation - Systems of the Body

Functions of the Body
III: Cooperation - Systems of the Body

Germ theory, antibiotics, and immunization
III: Cooperation - Systems of the Body (Immune)

TYPICAL COURSE OF STUDY* AND **KONOS****

GRADE 8

Social Studies

The U. S.
II: Early American History

Westward movement
III: Initiative/Resourcefulness - Frontier Life
I: Attentiveness - Frontiersmen/Tracking/Trapping

Civil War and Reconstruction
III: Cooperation - States and Regions

Growth and development of the United States
II: Wisdom - Government

The U.S. political system
II: Wisdom - Government and Presidents/Electoral Process

Exploring careers
I: Stewardship of Talents - Careers
Many other units

Science

Scientific method
II: Inquisitiveness - Scientists/Scientific Method

Magnetism and electricity
III: Initiative/Resourcefulness - Electricity and Magnetism

Composition of the earth
II: Inquisitiveness - The Earth

The ocean
II: Inquisitiveness - The Earth

Weather and atmosphere
II: Inquisitiveness - Weather

Space and space travel
I: Trust - Flight and Airplanes

Conservation
I: Stewardship of Natural Resources

Contributions of scientists
II: Inquisitiveness - Scientists/Scientific Method

Machines
III: Initiative/Resourcefulness - Simple Machines

The atom and chemical changes
III: Determination - Atomic Research

Mechanical, electrical, and nuclear energy
III: Initiative/Resourcefulness - Energy

Ecology, environment and recycling of resources
I: Stewardship of Natural Resources

Health and Safety

Safety
II: Wisdom - Safety

First aid
II: Wisdom - Safety

Types and functions of foods
I: Stewardship of the Body - Nutrition

Functions of the body
III: Cooperation - Systems of the Body

TYPICAL COURSE OF STUDY* AND **KONOS****
HIGH SCHOOL****

Social Studies	Government **II: Wisdom - Government**	Careers **I: Stewardship of Talents - Careers**
	Citizenship **II: Loyalty - Citizenship**	History of the world **KONOS History of the World (to be published, Lord willing!)**
	Economics **III: Honesty - Business**	American history **II: All units**
	Labor and management **III: Honesty - Business**	Current Affairs **II: Wisdom - Government**

Science

Earth science
II: Inquisitiveness - The Earth

Physical science - Air
I: Trust - Flight/Airplanes

Physical Science - Weather
II: Inquisitiveness - Weather

Physical Science - Electricity
III: Initiative/Resourcefulness - Electricity/Magnetism

Physical Science - Solar Energy
III: Initiative/Resourcefulness - Energy

Physical Science - Nuclear Energy
III: Initiative/Resourcefulness - Energy

Metals and Plastics
III: Initiative/Resourcefulness - Industrial Revolution/Inventions

Physical Science - Sound and Music
I: Attentiveness - Ears/Sound/Music

Physical Science - Machines
III: Initiative/Resourcefulness - Work and Simple Machines

Biology
Zoology
I: Orderliness - Animal Classification
I: Patience - Animal Birth and Growth

Botany
I: Orderliness - Plant Classification
I: Patience - Plant Birth and Growth

Genetics/Heredity
I: Honor/Respect - Individuality/Heredity

Human biology
III: Cooperation - Systems of the Body
I: Patience - Human Birth and Growth

Chemistry
III: Determination - Atomic Research

Physics - Mechanics
III: Initiative/Resourcefulness - Work and Simple Machines

Physics - Electricity and Magnetism
III: Initiative/Resourcefulness - Electricity and Magnetism

Physics - Sound and Acoustics
I: Attentiveness - Ears/Sound/Music

Physics - Light and Optics
I: Obedience - Authority/Light
I: Trust - Deception/Illusion

Physics - Force, work, energy, power
I: Obedience - Force/Friction
III: Initiative/Resourcefulness - Energy

Language/ Literature

Composition
See KONOS COMPASS - HOW DO I TEACH WRITING SKILLS?

Poetry
III: Self-control - Poetry

The Novel
III: Honesty - Books

Newspaper
III: Honesty - Newspapers and other media

Advertising
III: Honesty - Business/Advertising

Speech
III: Self-control - Speech

* *Typical Course of Study used with permission from World Book, Inc.*
** *KONOS Volumes revised 1989*
*** *See KONOS Math and Language Checklist*
**** *A foundation of learning; need to supplement for high school level*

WHAT IS NEEDED IN ADDITION TO KONOS?

Are you looking for the textbooks and workbooks? We do not provide any textbooks or workbooks for several reasons. First, we concentrate on experiential learning rather than textbook learning. The worst way to teach science is to use only textbooks; the best way is to experiment with real things. The worst way to teach history is to use only textbooks; the best way is to dramatize real people, "reliving" that period of history. Second, although we read extensively, we have intentionally chosen to use easy-to-get library books for information and for reading skills. Our recommended library books are of better literary and graphic quality than traditional textbooks. Your children will be exposed to classical literature, Newbery Award winners, and Caldecott Award winners. In addition, your children will become acquainted with how to use the library. For some books (e.g., Christian biographies) that cannot be found in your local library, we refer you to Christian bookstores. Third, we have a heart and a conscience to help home-schoolers. Assuming your library books are returned on time, there is absolutely no cost for the wonderful information you have at your fingertips.

We do use workbooks but only for math and language to reinforce particular skills. We have found little benefit to "filling in the blanks" when studying topics. In fact, they can actually decrease the learning potential of a child who might have the illusion of knowledge when in fact all he has done is to regurgitate data. We want our children to really *learn* what is covered, not just take it in, let it out on paper, and forget it. Within the KONOS volumes are many ideas of how to test your child's knowledge and reinforce what has been actually learned (e.g., oral quizzes, written tests, games).

Within the three volumes of KONOS are all the Bible, science, social studies, art, music, literature, health and safety that is required K-8. KONOS does *not* provide all that is needed in phonics, math, and language arts.

SUPPLEMENTING KONOS CURRICULUM		
Grade P - K	**Grade 1 - 3**	**Grade 4 - 8**
Phonics	Phonics Spelling Handwriting Math	Spelling Language Skills Math

Parents need to purchase a phonics program to teach their children to read. Sometime between kindergarten and second-grade, they need to start a spelling program, which they will continue throughout elementary school. A formal math program should be introduced sometime between kindergarten and second-grade level and continued until the child is ready for algebra. We recommend introducing a formal language arts program emphasizing punctuation, capitalization, grammar, and other language usage by second through fourth-grade level. Please refer to **HOW DO I SUPPLEMENT KONOS?** and **HOW DO I TEACH WRITING SKILLS?** See also the Math and Language Checklist under **WHAT SKILLS SHOULD MY CHILD ACCOMPLISH EACH YEAR?** These resources will assure you that your child is covering all the necessary skills.

MAY I SEE SOME SAMPLE PAGES?

The following are a few pages from the Patience Unit in Volume I. The Bible verses are to use for family devotions, Bible memory, and/or handwriting practice. Brackets ([ ]) after examples of people in each unit refers to the number of the figure on KONOS KIDS' TIMELINE FOR VOLUME I.

Vocabulary words are for parents to use in discussing animal growth with their children. Older children can use the words for a spelling and vocabulary list.

Numbers in parentheses after *Books* in the resource lists refer to Dewey Decimal numbers. After each book reference is the reading grade level of that book. Asterisks (*) in front of books in the resource lists refer to selections that we highly recommend. The more asterisks, the better we like it.

There are exciting, motivational activities from which to choose. The activities were designed to be multi-level so that several children of different ages in a family or co-op can do these activities together. If an activity is for a younger (K-2) child or an older child (6-8), we indicate that. Parents choose about half of the activities, selecting those that best fit their particular family's interests and needs. Don't be concerned about not choosing the *right* activites. *All* the activities are *right* but might not be *preferred* by you. A good rule of thumb in making the decision on what to choose is "What would my child *enjoy* doing and what would make this topic *real* to him?"

ANIMAL BIRTH/GROWTH UNIT

Some animals' growth periods are short while others are longer. This seems to correspond to the species life span. Nevertheless, growth requires waiting, and waiting requires patience. God does everything in His own time.

1. BIBLE

   Ps. 37:7 Rest in the Lord and be patient for Him.

2. EXAMPLES

   Animals
   Jane Goodall [73]

3. VOCABULARY

   Chicken
   embryology
   incubator
   imprinting

   brooding
   germ cell

   incubate
   brood patch

   Insect
   metamorphosis
   scales
   head
   spiracles

   transform
   chitin
   thorax
   compound eye

   antennae
   proboscis
   abdomen

   Developmental Stages (Insects)
   egg
   chrysalis

   caterpillar
   pupa

   cocoon
   butterfly

   Frog/Toad
   egg
   toad
   lungs
   wart
   algae

   frog
   amphibian
   breathing skin
   croak
   hibernate

   tadpole or "pollywog"
   gills
   paritoid gland
   vocal sac

   Dragonfly
   egg

   nymph

   adult

   Fish
   spawning
   skate
   yolk sac

   roe
   sperm

   milt
   fry

   Mammals/Marsupials
   snuggle
   colostrum
   tactile

   nuzzle
   cuddle
   life expectance

   grooming
   bonding
   generation

286

4. RESOURCES

   a. Books

**** The Amazing Egg, by Robert M. McClung (Factual, informative book about the many varieties of eggs) (Gr. 4-9)

Metamorphasis: The Magic Change by Alwin and Virginia Silverstein (Covers the startling developments in frogs, butterflies, etc.) (Gr. 3-7)

What's Hatching Out of That Egg by Patricia Lauber (Excellent pictures and text) (Gr. 2-6)

Lillies, Rabbits, and Painted Eggs The Story of the Easter Symbols by Edna Barth (Explanation of many of the Easter symbols and their origins.) (Gr. 3-6)

* An Egg is For Wishing by Helen Kay (A Ukranian boy is afraid of the rooster and will not get a chicken egg for his mother to make a pysanka) (Gr. P-3)

* About Eggs and Creatures that Hatch from Them by Melvin John Uhl (Amphibians, birds, insects, mammals) (Gr. 1-5)

Eggshells to Objects by Susan Riser Arnold (Art projects) (Gr. 1-7)

** Eggs and What Happens Inside Them by Margaret Cosgrove (Many kinds of animals; experimentation with why eggs develop certain ways) (Gr. 3-7)

Window into an Egg by Geraldine Lux Flanagan (Gr. 2-6)

**** Inside an Egg by Sylvia A. Johnson (Outstanding presentation of development of chicken egg; Children's Science Book Award winner) (Gr. 1-6)

Little Chicks Story by Mary DeBall Kwitz (Easy reader) (Gr. K-3)

** Butterflies and Moths by MacDonald Educational (Great information; easy reader) (Gr. K-4)

I Like Caterpillars by Gladys Conklin (Easy reader; shows different caterpillars) (Gr. K-2)

** Butterflies and Moths by Rosamund Kidman Cox (Great; easy) (Gr. K-3)

** Caterpillars and How They Live by Robert M. McClung (Loads of information) (Gr. 2-6)

Butterflies and Moths: How They Function by Dorothy Hinshaw Patent (Complete) (Gr. 5-9)

Monarch Butterfly by Marion Marcher (Good information; easy to read) (Gr. K-3)

Luna: The Story of a Moth by Robert M. McClung (Easy reader) (Gr. K-3)

* Butterflies by Dorothy Childs Hogner (Easy to read) (Gr. 2-4)

* Moths by Dorothy Childs Hogner (Easy to read) (Gr. 2-4)

Monarch Butterflies by Peter Burchard (Complete; good information) (Gr. 3-7)

** The Travels of Monarch X by Ross E. Hutchins (Great information and true story of a tagged Monarh; easy to read) (Gr. 2-5)

*** Caterpillars by Dorothy Sterling (Great information; cleverly written) (Gr. 1-6)

** Fireflies in the Night by Kazue Mizummura (Cute story with information) (Gr. P-2)

** Metamorphosis: The Magic Change by Alwin and Virginia Silverstein (Good pictures and information on moths, bees, dragonflies, starfish, eels, sea squirts) (Gr. 2-7)

** The Story Book of Silk by Maud and Miska Petersham (An excellent husband-wife team authors) (Gr. 2-6)

* Let's Learn About Silk by Maud and Miska Petersham (Gr. 2-6)

**** Silkworms by Sylvia Johnson (Fabulous photogrphs and information) (Gr. 1-6)

Silkworms and Science by Elizabeth K. Cooper (Complete; informative) (Gr. 4-8)

** Collecting Cocoons by Lois Hussey (Very good identification of cocoons and "how-to-do-it" information) (Gr. 2-8)

The Insects World by John Pallister (Lists insects by the months they appear; good information) (Gr. 3-6)
* Let's Look at Insects by Harriet Huntington (Very good information and photography) (Gr. 2-7)
The True Book of Insects by Illa Podendorf (Easy reader) (Gr. K-3)
Let's Find Out about Insects by David C. Knight (Easy reader) (Gr. K-3)
** Discovering Insects by Grenn O. Blough (Good overall picture of insects) (Gr. 2-6)
Insects and Their Young by Rosse Hutchins (Complete and detailed) (Gr. 4-8)
Insects all Around Us by Richard Armour (Cleverly written poetry about many insects; illustrated by Paul Galdone) (Gr. P-3)
A First Look at Spiders by Millicent E. Selsam and Joyce Hunt (Gr. K-4)
The Story of Spiders by Dorothy Shuttlesworth (Great information) (Gr. 3-8)
Spiders by Illa Podendorf (Easy) (Gr. P-2)
Spiders by Phyllis Jean Perry (Easy) (Gr. P-2)
Spider Magic by Dorothy Hinshaw Patent (Good photographs and information) (Gr. 2-6)
** Spiders and How They Live by Eugene David (Very good overall picture of spiders) (Gr. 2-6)
* Frogs and Polliwogs by Dorothy Childs Hogner (Gr. 2-5)
*** Frogs and Toads by Jane Dallinger (Great pictures; a Natural Science Book) (Gr. 1-7)
* The Life Cycle of Frog by Paula Hogan (Easy to read; good illustrations) (Gr. P-3)
Frogs and Toads by Herbert S. Zim (Easy to read; good information) (Gr. 2-4)
** Frogs Toads and Newts by Francis Ommanny (Very unusual behavior of frogs; well written) (Gr. 2-8)
Spring Peepers by Judy Hawes (Gr. P-2)
A First Look at Frogs, Toads and Salamanders by Millicent E. Selsam and Joyce Hunt (Great) (Gr. P-5)
* Why Frogs Are Wet by Judy Hawes (Easy; informative) (Gr. P-3)
* Getting Born by Russell Freedman (Good photographs; animal reproduction) (Gr. 1-6)
* The First Days of Life by Russell Freedman (Relates early animal behavior of fish, turtles, chicks, wolves, dolphins, chimpanzees) (Gr. 3-6)
**** How Life Begins: A Look at Birth and Care in the Animal World by Chrissy Rankin (Wonderful text and fabulous photographs) (Gr. K-6)

b. Other

Bullfrogs and Butterflies, Sparrow Records, Inc. 8587 Canoga Ave., Canoga Park, CA 91304 (Gr. P-adult)

5. ACTIVITIES   · Science

a. Catch a caterpillar and raise it to a moth or butterfly. To find one, look for leaves chewed and silk strands or webs. Look on walnuts, hickorys, ailanthus, rose bushes, mulberrys, milkweeds, wild-cherry trees and Virginia Creepers. (See Caterpillars by Dorothy Sterling) For a cage an ordinary glass jar or box will do. Caterpillars need very little air, no sun at all, lots of fresh leaves to eat and a twig to climb on.

288

Gather the leaves you found it on. You must clean its cage everyday of droppings and withered leaves or it will get sick. Other cages are flower pots full of dirt or dampened peat moss, so the leaves will stay fresh, and a chimney lamp cover or inverted jar. Caterpillars can be left outside by sewing a muslin sleeve to slip over the branch and tie at each end. Move the sleeve as needed. Watch for molting and spinning in the figure-eight pattern.

b. Make a butterfly net and catch insects. Observe and let go or start an insect collection.

c. Read about the Monarch butterfly and its life. Plot its travels on a map. (See The Travels of Monarch X by Ross E. Hutchins). How far did the butterrflies fly? Why do you think the Monarch flew along the east coast and not over the mountains?

d. Sing "Bullfrogs and Butterflies" (See resource list). What is the religious meaning of this song?

e. On newspaper or manilla paper folded in half and then open, drop or apply several random shaped and spaced blobs of tempera color on one side of the fold only. Now fold the paper back along the fold and rub to make a mirror image. Open and drop a different colored blob, repeating the process. Can you see a butterfly or anything? Paint an outline to finish your design.

f. Make a critter cage.

g. Read about unusual moths in Scaly Wings by Ross E. Hutchins. The yucca plant can only be pollinated by the yucca moth. And the yucca moth's caterpillars eat the seeds of the yucca plant. Mexican jumping beans are really seed pods of plants with small caterpillars living in them. When wrmed they flip about. Get some Mexican jumping beans and look inside.

h. Paint a butterfly with tempera paints sitting on a sunny flower.

i. Using body movements and soft butterfly music (see list of woodwind music in Attentiveness, Volume I) create a butterfly dance. You may want to even design and create your own wings.

j. Read about the Chinese Empress Si-Ling-Chi who was drinking tea in the garden when one of her servants gave her a cocoon to look at. It accidentally fell into her teacup. When she got it out, the cocoon was soft and had started to unwind. Dramatize her story and how China came to produce silk.

- Arts/Crafts
- Science

- Geography
- Math
- Reasoning

- Music

- Arts/Crafts

- Science

- Arts/Crafts

- Music
- Creative Expression
- Arts/Crafts

- History
- Social Studies
- Creative Expression

289

k. Write a paper on silk production entitled <u>From Cocoon to Silk Cloth.</u> Notice how the silk worm has become so domesticated that its legs have become undeveloped because it has not had to move around and find food.

- Social Studies
- Language

l. Find a cocoon and soak it in boiling water for a few minutes. Now with tweezers try to unwind the silk.

- Social Studies
- Fun

m. Tent caterpillars and webworms live in a nest of silk. Find some of these and observe them even at night with a flashlight. When do they eat? Write up your observations.

- Science
- Language

n. Learn which caterpillars change into which moths or butterflies; which caterpillars are poisonous; how they protect themselves; how they spin silk. After you have learned this share it with your father at dinner.

- Science
- Language

o. Make a butterfly by cutting two thicknesses of wax paper in the shape of a butterfly's wings:

- Arts/Crafts

Grate different colored crayons and sprinkle between the two sheets of waxed paper. Iron with a warm iron. Cut a body out of paper or fold a pipe cleaner. Let the antennae extend. Hang from wire or thread in a window.

p. Catch a moth and a butterfly and compare them. Look at antennae, wings and how wings are folded. What about tongues? Can you see their scales? Write about your observations.

- Science
- Language

q. Read about the metamorphosis of the dragonfly (See: <u>Metamorphosis: The Magic Change</u> by Alvin and Virginia Silverstein. There are different stages of development from the butterfly. Explain the developmental stages of these two in a paper.

- Science
- Language

r. It takes the chicken egg twenty-one days to hatch. The chick cannot get any food or water from the outside. How does it live? Go to a chicken farm or to a friend's farm and bring home a fertilized egg. Are the eggs we eat usually fertilized?

- Practical Living
- Character
- Science
- Fun

290

Before going to the farm research chicken incubation and set up your own incubator. Be sure you're able to maintain the proper temperature. Make detailed notes about the hatching process. Part of God's provision is for each chick to know when to peck and where to find its way into the world. Were you patient waiting for the chick to hatch? What would happen if you tried to hatch an unfertilized egg? You would really need patience for that!

• Science
• Theology

s. Examine a chicken egg. Do you know you are looking at an unfertilized ovum? Crack the egg open and look for the three main parts, the shell, the yolk, and the white. These three distinct parts are all necessary to form one whole egg. This might be an excellent opportunity to talk about the one God of the universe, but with three distinct parts.

• Science

t. Look at the shell of an egg through a magnifying glass. Can air pass in and out of the shell? Why or why not?

• Physical Skills
• Science
• Fun

u. Try spinning a boiled egg on its base and a raw egg on its base. What is the difference and why? Can you design a trick to trick members of your family?

• Theology

v. How is God like an egg? Explain how God is three in one just as the egg is a shell, yolk, and albumen.

• Literature

w. Read an _Egg is For Wishing_ about pysanky eggs.

• Arts/Crafts

x. Make pysanky eggs, a Ukrainian tradition. Pysanky means "to write," and the eggs are decorated with all kinds of lines and symbols. You will need a special tool called a kistka which consists of a stylus and a funnel part for holding a small amount of beeswax. The wax is kept liquid by the flame of a candle. For instructions, pysanky dyes, and a kistka consult a Russian or Greek orthodox church sales-room or a crafts supply shop. This is a wonderful Easter tradition to make these and give them as gifts.

A single egg is **pysanka**.

Many eggs are **pysanky**.

 A flower means **love**.

 A pine tree is for **health**.

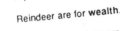 Reindeer are for **wealth**.

 Hens and **roosters** are for wishes coming true.

 A **spiral** stands for growing.

WHAT RESULTS CAN I EXPECT USING KONOS?

Although children who are taught the KONOS way tend to excel academically, there are many factors to consider. We do not know what kind of teacher you are. We do not know how experienced you are in using these methods. What are your children like? Are there any learning disabilities?

Perhaps the best way to measure is to plot a curve comparing your child's scores before and after using KONOS. By comparing these results, you will see that the KONOS methods are the way your child best learns.

But academic excellence is not the only thing we are teaching. We are training in biblical character. Are you a good character role model for your children? Unfortunately, if you are impatient, your children will follow your example and be impatient also. How do we measure character development? Suppose you as a mother want to know how patient you are. What is the best way to find out? Why, ask your husband, of course. In the same way, the best way to measure the character development of a child is to observe his behaviors within the family. Is he kinder? Neater? More obedient? More generous? More responsible? No child will *master* wisdom after the Wisdom unit, but he should know what wisdom is, how to make wise choices, and actually start practicing being wise. You should see a marked, positive change in his behavior.

KONOS is designed to build thinking skills in children, but how is that measured? When our children were first required to figure out things themselves, such as the baker's hat, the most common response was tears. With time, however, they have gained a confidence that they can, in fact, figure something out. They can break a big problem down into parts and consider the resources they have at hand to help them solve a problem. Their creative energy has maximized and they have become more independent learners without having to be "spoon-fed." Observe your child's reasoning ability before and after using KONOS. You should see a significant increase in his ability to solve problems and to create.

In addition to advancement in academics, moral development, and reasoning skill, you can expect to see a more enthusiastic learner. Children who were once bored with the learning process realize that learning can be fun. As M.K. of Texas stated, *"My children love learning again. Praise the Lord! I don't have to fight to motivate."* If your children beg you to do KONOS, you can be sure you are producing children who love learning. You are creating life-time learners.

14

WHO?

WHO WROTE KONOS?

Jessica Hulcy and Carole Thaxton are both trained teachers. After majoring in English and biology, and doing master's work in zoology and education, Jessica found herself doing what she loves best—teaching. For four years she taught physical science and biology to children in the ghetto where nobody wanted to be in school, nobody could read, and there were no resources. It was there without the aid of textbooks or workbooks that she realized that children learn best by doing and discovering. Her fifth year she taught in a "privileged" school where she found that her honor students and average students also learned better by doing and discovery. Meanwhile, Jessica's husband Wade taught history and physical education, coached and principaled before he moved to the business world. Both Wade and Jessica had first-hand experiences with public schools as well as ideas on <u>how</u> they wanted their own children taught. When they became Christians, they then knew <u>what</u> they wanted their children to learn. After meeting Carole and Charles, they became convinced that they wanted to home-school their children.

Carole was certified to teach secondary biology and chemistry. Shortly after becoming a Christian, she received a master's degree in counseling. Her years of counseling have included working with students "after the fact." Many of her clients had burnt out on learning, primarily because they had been mistaught. Carole married Charles, who received a Ph.D. in physical chemistry. Although he had been <u>highly</u> educated, he did not consider himself <u>well</u> educated. He was a specialist in his field, but he had not been taught the "big picture." He excelled in his academic study, but he had inadequate practical living skills. Both Charles and Carole determined that when they had children they would give them God's big picture, training in true godliness, and practical living skills. In 1982 they took the plunge and began teaching their own children.

Wade and Jessica, neighbors of the Thaxtons, finally "gave in" and also decided to teach their sons at home. Since the two families agreed wholeheartedly with "the KONOS way," they incorporated as The KONOS Academy. Jessica and Carole taught the children by day and wrote lesson plans by night. Once they knew what God wanted as a framework, the ideas began flowing (and have not yet stopped!). They taught them to their own children and saw them work. The activities that they did became well-known locally and began to spread nationally.

Never intending to have a business, in 1984 they published KONOS CHARACTER CURRICULUM for other families to use. They were stunned by its immediate and enthusiastic acceptance. "This is what home schooling is all about," exclaimed C.L. of Oklahoma. It was so well-received that Volumes II and III were published, completing the elementary school curriculum. Timelines were produced to be used with each volume. A KONOS KIDS' TIMELINE OF BIBLICAL CHARACTERS and a KONOS KIDS' TIMELINE OF ARTISTS AND COMPOSERS were also published. Cassette tapes entitled HOW TO USE KONOS CURRICULUM and BUILDING A GOOD WRITER THE KONOS WAY were recorded from live seminars to help families get started in the KONOS way.

The Hulcys and the Thaxtons continue to teach their children, excited about their moral and academic progress. Their sincere hope is to help other parents to meet their goals in training up their children (Col. 1:10).

WHAT IS YOUR STATEMENT OF FAITH?

1) We believe in one sovereign God, creator of all things, existing in three persons—Father, Son, and Holy Spirit.

2) We believe the Bible to be the inspired, infallible Word of God.

3) We believe that all have sinned and have fallen short of the glory of God. The only way to be reconciled to the Father is through belief in His Son, Jesus Christ, who died as a substitution on our behalf.

WHY?

WHY WAS KONOS WRITTEN?

KONOS did not start out as a business. It was started by two families with a vision of what God wanted for their children. When we started writing curriculum, we had in mind three goals. These are still our goals. We want our children to:

1) Have godly character

We want children who are Christians, dedicated to pleasing God with their lives. We want them to cooperate with the Holy Spirit in having their characters transformed into the same character as Jesus Christ's. This includes knowing what is true, seeking what is good, and doing what is right.

2) Be fully equipped for life

We want our children not only to be good, but to be thoroughly equipped to do God's work in this world. To adequately have dominion over the earth, they must gain necessary skills. These include academic skills like a workable knowledge of math, interesting and persuasive writing skills, reading appreciation and comprehension, and a true perspective of what God and people have done in history. But being thoroughly equipped also includes such practical living skills as relating to other people, knowing one's own strengths and weaknesses, choosing wise friends, doing laundry, knowing basic auto mechanics, cooking nutritionally, and even loving little brother. In addition, to be equipped to do God's will in this world, one must be a thinking Christian. We want children who can make good judgments, can solve problems, and can make creative contributions to this world.

3) Love learning

We want our children to love learning and to be motivated to keep learning all their lives. We want to keep that sparkle in their eyes as they discover more of God's truth. Children who are not enthusiastic about learning are a poor testimony of God's wonder, whereas an enthusiastic learner is a witness of God's hope and joy.

WHY DID YOU CHOOSE YOUR PARTICULAR CONTENT AND METHODS?

We chose content and methods to meet our goals. Although not responsible for the result of how our children respond, we are responsible for how we train them. If we want to train our children in godly character, do we teach everything but character? Or do we teach about character without any opportunity to practice these qualities? Of course not. If we want our children to be fully equipped in both academic and practical living skills, do we teach only academics? Of course not. If we want children that are becoming thinking Christians, do we fail to challenge their creative, problem-solving ability? Of course not. If we want enthusiastic learners, do we use primarily a textbook-workbook approach? Of course not.

Content

The content of KONOS is oriented around Biblical character qualities. Why? God has told us parents to instruct our children in character first. Therefore, the focal point of our curriculum is character development. Deuteronomy 6:1-6 clearly instructs parents to concentrate on developing moral behavior in their children. If we, as parents, do not teach good character, like honoring authorities, generosity, responsibility, and self-control, who will do it for us? The Lord will hold us accountable for instructing or not instructing our children.

We agree with Paul in his letter to Timothy that the goal of our instruction is "a pure heart, a good conscience, and a sincere faith" (1 Tim. 1:5). In other words, the purpose of teaching our children is the development of Christ-like character. Just this week I called two different women to clean our house. The first took down my address and promised to arrive at noon the next day. She never arrived and never called. I called her several times during the following days, but only received word from a babysitter that she had returned to school. She has yet to return my calls. The second woman promised to arrive at one o'clock today. It is now three o'clock and no word. I called her home only to find that their phone had been disconnected. Is this surprising? No, except that both of these women are professing Christians. We have heard them speak about their love for the Lord, yet their character is inconsistent. This should not be. We are ambassadors for Jesus Christ. Our children must be taught to "walk the faith" not just "talk the faith."

KONOS' curriculum content seeks to make our children aware of God's standard for character. This, of course, is revealed in Scripture. Our children become further accquainted with character traits, as they recognize, identify, discern, and zero in on them in the lives of people that KONOS provides as examples. Except for Jesus, not one of our examples is perfectly righteous; some of our examples are not even Christians. Just because someone is a Christian does not mean that he will always exhibit godly character. Likewise, just because someone is not a Christian does not mean that he will not exhibit godly character. We want our children to measure character against God's standard, not base it on who did it.

Do we expect that at the end of each unit the child has mastered that character trait? No. Just because a child has studied patience does not mean that he will be patient. This is true for at least three reasons. As we have stated before, child development depends upon the modeling of these behaviors by respected adults. Therefore, it is so important that the whole family be growing in Christian character. Secondly, character development is a life-long, gradual process and is not grasped once for all. Thirdly, Christian character development is more than merely understanding a principle and applying it; it is a Holy Spirit-inspired devotion to goodness. As one grows in relationship with God, the fruits of the Spirit grow likewise. Given these three qualifications, however, character can and ought to be taught. While we are not responsible for what our children choose to do as adults, we are responsible to instruct them in righteousness.

It is also our responsibility as parents to train our children in life skills. KONOS is not just a character-building curriculum; it is a skill-building curriculum designed to fully equip our children for life. With KONOS, boys and girls grow in their knowledge, skill, and appreciation of science, social studies, art, music, health, literature, writing, and practical living skills. All this is done from a biblical perspective to give them a firm base in being God's people in this world.

Methods

Identifying and discerning godly character is only the first half of acquiring it. Knowing what it is does not mean being able to apply it. Therefore, KONOS is interested not only in the content of what is taught but also the method of how it is taught. KONOS' way to instill character in children is to provide mounds of activities that "force" children to practice the character trait. Children are not merely told to be responsible, they are given opportunities to actually practice responsibility, thereby internalizing the character trait.

To maximize our teaching, we want to use all the methods that are consistent with the way God made children. KONOS, therefore, employs the methods of unit studies, experiential learning, discovery learning, and multi-level learning. These methods help us to achieve our goals for our children—having godly character, being fully equipped with skills, and loving learning.
After years of research, experts know how children best learn. Parents observe the same things just by being parents. The chart below indicates their findings:

HOW CHILDREN BEST LEARN

YOUNGER	MIDDLE	OLDER
General (Unit Studies)	⟶	**Specific**
Concrete (Experiential Learning)	⟶	**Abstract**
Understanding (Discovery Learning)	⟶	**Mastery**
Nourishing Environment (Multi-level Home Learning)	⟶	**Society**

The chart shows gradual movement from the left side of the chart to the right side. Children learn best when they are first given broad, general, unified themes and then progress to more specialized study. Of what value, for instance, is the date 1752, the "birth" of the Liberty Bell, if the children have no concept of B.C. and A.D. and no understanding of the approximate time of the Revolutionary War. Far better to have a general understanding and to gradually move toward more specific dates. Secondly, children learn best when given concrete, real-life experiences and then progress to abstract reasoning. How do children understand an abstract principle like "The Lord is my shepherd?" The best way is to have exposure to a concrete, real-life shepherd. Thirdly, children learn best after given genuine understanding of a concept and then progress to mastery of that concept. Is it possible to master a concept if it isn't understood? Of course not, yet think of how often that happens in the teaching of math. Far better to give children a working knowledge of a math concept (e.g., adding money spent to prepare a meal) before doing drills on money addition. Lastly, children learn best in a nourishing educational environment, from which they gradually progress to well-functioning adults in society. How can we expect true moral development if it is not practiced within the family unit? For every character trait that we study there is ample opportunity to practice that trait within the family. The children learn together, reinforcing what they learn and enjoying the relationships within the family while gradually being exposed to society.

KONOS CURRICULUM is designed around these methods—unit studies (integrated learning), experiential learning, discovery learning, and multi-level home learning. We did this to teach children in the way they best learn.

UNIT STUDIES (INTEGRATED LEARNING)

Most learning that lasts is interdisciplinary. This is accomplished by taking a whole unit, like North American Indians, owls, ancient Olympics, or the American Revolution and approaching it in a general, unified way. Integrating the various subject matter provides genuine motivation to learn, encourages better recall, and is more interesting. Isolated subjects usually fail to interest the child, fail to reinforce each other and fail to provide any reason for learning. In fact, by teaching isolated subjects, the child is more easily distracted from real learning. Unified themes excite the child and maximize teaching efforts. Because our goal is to shape our children in godly character, we have designed the curriculum around character traits we want to develop. All of the resources and activities were chosen to reinforce each of these traits. Therefore, all the subject-matter (Bible, art, music, language arts, science, social studies, health and safety, writing, and practical living) is integrated around a character trait theme. Each theme is reinforced by activities using different subjects. For example, with the theme of Patience, we baked bread (math, practical living), made baker's hats (craft, math), studied the life of Jacob (reading, history), experimented with yeast (science), searched the Bible for references to bread (Bible), and studied homophones like "knead/need," "flour/ flower," "whole/hole," "bread/bred," and "sew/so" (language arts).

The KONOS KIDS' TIMELINES are also wonderful teachers of the "big picture." Students learn the general placement of people in history. Moving from the general, students are later ready to concentrate and specialize. When Jason was nine years old he was placing all of the explorers on the Timeline and noticed they all had telescopes. As he placed the settlers on the Timeline, he noticed they all had hatchets. Likewise, the Revolutionary War figures all had three-pointed hats, and the founding fathers all had white wigs. Stepping back, he viewed his work and a "light went on." "Oh, I see. The telescopes are in the 1500's so that's the exploring time; the hatchets are in the 1600's so that's the settling time; and in the 1700's we became a nation. That's easy!" And he is right. Later he will be encouraged to know specific dates.

EXPERIENTIAL LEARNING

In response to the current problem of lowered academic proficiency, there is a trend in education that is a departure from traditional educational practice. The trend is toward introducing abstract learning concepts at an even earlier age. The assumption is that by introducing certain abstract concepts earlier they will be learned better. But earlier does not equal better. Head Start[1] and other pilot projects have demonstrated this. Children have not become better readers by introducing the alphabet earlier, have not used mathematics better by introducing drill cards earlier, and have not become better writers by completing language workbooks earlier.

While agreeing that older children today are less proficient in abstract skills than in previous years, the KONOS solution to this problem is different. We choose to raise the age of abstract skill development instead of lowering it and to use these earlier years to provide more concrete, real-life, hands-on, multi-sensory experiences. Providing concrete experiences with much manipulation of tangible objects over a prolonged time in a real environment is the only demonstrated way to develop abstract skills.

The following illustrates how a child progresses from the concrete to the abstract. Our three-year-old is learning the concept of the number "5" by setting the table with five spoons, five forks, five knives, five plates, etc. Later, when he is introduced to the symbol "5" it will have meaning and will be usable. Our five-year-old son, on the other hand, is comprehending the meaning of addition by manipulating match box cars. Although he can now perform on command "5 + 4 = 9",

---

[1] Waller, D. A. and Conners, C. K., 1966. A follow-up study of intelligence changes in children who participated in Project Head Start. ED 020 786, 1966.

he is still referring to tangible objects like cars, blocks, or fingers when he makes this calculation. He will eventually wean himself away from concrete experiences to abstract thinking.

KONOS is a hands-on curriculum filled with concrete activities to do. Our curriculum puts life into learning through experiential activities. We have admittedly overemphasized experiential learning in hopes of bringing the educational "see-saw" back in balance. While we do subscribe to the necessity of seatwork and drillwork, we do not consider these to be the major emphasis of true education. In our curriculum you will note many multi-sensory, participatory activities.

In Volume II, for example, while studying Wisdom, Carole worked with the older boys. They dressed like George Washington (three-cornered hats, cotton wigs, knickers), learned how to plot and survey like Washington did, re-enacted the Revolutionary War, and discussed the wisdom of Washington's tactical decisions. In the car on the way home from the field trip, they worked crossword puzzles of Revolutionary War facts. Meanwhile, Jessica read D'Aulaire's George Washington to the younger boys, asked neighbors to dance the minuet with them, dramatized a fox hunt after a stray dog ("Tally ho and away!"), discussed the wisdom of taking snuff, and "crossed the Delaware" (on a log pile with stick oars). The activities in our curriculum are designed to internalize, i.e., to make real, whatever the child is learning and to have fun doing it.

DISCOVERY LEARNING

We believe that a concept must first be understood to be mastered. Any normal child can memorize. Since he enjoys repetition, he will easily recite whatever he is assigned—the alphabet, math drill cards, or the Declaration of Independence. The question is not whether a child can memorize proficiently. The question is whether by doing this he is gaining mastery of the concept.

Consider the following examples. By memorizing the chronology of presidents, will the child better understand what a president is? By memorizing the Twenty-third Psalm, will the child better understand the relationship between a shepherd and the Lord? By practicing fraction drill cards, will he better understand the concept of fractions? True understanding of a concept prepares the child for mastery; mastery (i.e. memory and other refinement skill) does not promote understanding.

The development of true understanding requires active, personal, mental involvement (e.g. imagining, generalizing, comparing, evaluating) plus time. The child needs freedom to explore his environment. In fact, the parent can sometimes serve his child best by giving him ample time to explore his environment and to discover the nature of the world rather than by "teaching" him.[2] A child who is allowed to explore is led to new encounters with people and things, ever widening his learning potential. The child also develops reasoning skills through asking questions about first-hand experiences, through creating on his own, through trying new methods, and even through failing.

By using discovery learning, we are encouraging a child to teach himself. In spite of the child's need for adult guidance, by interjecting unneeded and unsolicited advice, a child may not only reject learning but may reject his teacher as well. "A word to the wise is...infuriating!"[3]

The following illustrates how a child progresses from understanding a concept to mastery and

2 Gesell, A. and Ilg, F. L., Infant and Child in the Culture of Today, NY, Harper & Row, 1943

3 Holt, John, Teach Your Own, NY, Dell Publishing Co., Inc., 1981, p. 211.

refinement of skills. At five years, Jason "discovered" fractions by measuring volumes of flour ("Oh, I see, 4/4s is a whole cup; 3/3s is a whole cup."). This does not mean, however, that he had mastered fractions. He merely understood the concept but had not mastered addition, substraction, and multiplication of them. That would come later.

Compare this with John Holt's experience teaching fifth graders fractions. He had been asking questions like "If you had three candy bars and wanted to divide them evenly among five people, how would you do it?". Most of the children could think of at least one way to do it. Then they "had" fractions. Interestingly, the childern could no longer solve the problems. They had not yet sufficiently understood the concept. Instead of applying their ingenuity to problem-solving, they were trying to fit the problem into the "rules" they had learned.[4] If they had been encouraged, instead, to keep figuring on their own as Holt was encouraging, they would have generalized to certain short-cuts. Thus they would have extrapolated to the "rules" and would have been able to use them when necessary and appropriate.

As these examples show, it takes adequate development of reasoning skills for the child to be prepared for true mastery of concepts. A child must learn to think for true mastery of knowledge to take place. Of course it would be easier to hand our children a list of assignments to do at their desks. But what do we really want for our children—the ability to fill in blanks or the ability to think? If you do not want to invest your time and energy in producing real thinkers, then this curriculum is not for you.

Education is more than just learned content; it is the development of reasoning skills. For this reason, we have included activities conducive to discovery techniques. We encourage the child to figure things out on his own. Remember, while studying Attentiveness, we visited the zoo aviary to observe birds, being attentive to their distinctive beaks and feet. The children inferred that birds with short, fat beaks eat nuts and grains whereas those with long beaks usually eat fish. When making baker's hats, we could have merely demonstrated how to make one. To be more challenging we could have given them a pattern to make their own hats. But wanting to stretch their "reasoning muscles", we showed them a picture of a baker's hat and asked them to figure out how to make one. Does it take longer to teach in this way? Yes. Is it worth it? Yes. Dictatorships are always more efficient, but they do not produce creative, reasoning people.

Many of these activities take place on our Discovery Day (KONOS co-op day), which we have once a week. We give the children opportunity to observe and to ask questions on their own. We believe that it is more important for them to ask their own questions than for them to answer our questions. Our role during this time is to guide. There is an old saying that a mediocre teacher tells, a good teacher explains, a great teacher shows, but the greatest teacher leads, directs, challenges, and inspires.

Of course not everything can be discovered through the child's own reasoning process. Ultimate truths are reserved for the authority of Scripture. But without some opportunity for a child to discover on his own, he will not develop thinking skills.

MULTI-LEVEL HOME LEARNING

Environment can foster learning or stifle it. Therefore, the learning environment we choose for our children should provide for optimal education. Recent research has indicated that school, i.e.

---

[4] Ibid., p. 216

formal group instruction, is best suited for later elementary years.[5] For primary age children, the home is the best context for effective learning.

The home, on the one hand, provides a microcosm of the real world where a child must recognize and respond to the various needs of different people of different ages. He learns patience while listening to a grandparent and learns responsibility in caring for a younger sibling. His whole personality is being developed as he shifts from leader, to follower, to one of the gang. He is not in, what Charlotte Mason terms, the isolated "child environment" which is totally child-centered.

On the other hand, the home provides a nourishing, nurturing environment in which a child's identity and security take deep roots as loving, permanent relationships with family members develop. The result is a feeling of safety. Susan Schaeffer Macaulay points out in her book For the Children's Sake that children can play "camping" quite creatively and independently under a tree for hours, while they have the assurance that a watchful adult is nearby. We encourage their freedom within the constraints of safety. "They are independent, yes, but with the freedom of being in a pasture, not the danger of hiking alone through the mountaintops."[6]

Members of the family unit share the same Christian values. As these values are consistently reinforced, the child feels secure and grows in character.

Children realize that education is not static. It is a growing process to be shared with others and to be cultivated in their own lives. Education is not something acquired once for all. It is an ongoing life-long process.

Multi-leveled learning within the home context allows children to learn in ways that will prepare them to be well-equipped, life-long learners, becoming productive, giving members of society.

SUMMARY OF CONTENT AND METHODS

KONOS was written to meet the goals of what we really want for our children. We meet our goals through unique content and methods. The five distinctives of the KONOS CHARACTER CURRICULUM, unit studies around character trait themes (integrated subjects), experiential learning, discovery learning, and multi-level home learning are five teaching methods which help us teach our children the way they best learn. Through these methods we meet our goals of developing strong Christian character, excellence in equipping skills, and life-time learning.

WHY SHOULD I USE KONOS?

You shouldn't use KONOS unless your goals are the same as ours. You must consider what you really want for your children. We have told you what our goals are. What are your goals? If you agree with our three main goals of building Christians of godly character, fully equipping your children to do God's work in this world, and creating life-time learners who are motivated to keep pursuing God, then evaluate curriculum according to these goals.

---

[5] Moore, Raymond S. and Dorothy N., School Can Wait, Provo, Utah, Brigham Young University Press, 1979

[6] Macaulay, Susan Schaeffer, For the Children's Sake, Crossway Books, Westchester, Ill., 1984, p. 53.

Does the curriculum train godly character?
Is there opportunity to actually put into practice what is learned?
Are the methods consistent with the way God made children?
Are unit studies used so that the children can see how the pieces fit into a whole?
Is there sufficient hands-on, experiential activity?
Do the children retain what they learn?
Are the children challenged to think?
Can the whole family use the curriculum together?
Do the activities promote an appetite for learning?
Do the children have fun?
Is there enough *form* to provide structure yet enough *freedom* to adapt to
   our family's needs?

As expressed in **WHAT RESULTS CAN I EXPECT USING KONOS?**, KONOS kids are excelling academically and morally. Not only are they learning well, but they have an excitement about learning. Although we believe KONOS is the *best* curriculum to use, it is not the *easiest* curriculum to use. It does demand time, effort, and personal involvement with your children. Do not use it unless you believe it is God's best for your family. It is much easier to put a child at a desk with a list of assignments. Although we believe in seatwork for a portion of our children's training, we know that quality education is not primarily *textbook-taught;* it is *teacher-taught*. Only you can make the decision of whether your children merit this investment.

In E.B. White's <u>Charlotte's Web</u>, Wilbur, the pig, asks the dying spider what she is making in her web. Charlotte answers that she is working on her "magnum opus," her greatest work, her egg sac. We believe like Charlotte that each of our children is a magnum opus, our greatest work to give back to the Lord. Is he worth it? You bet!

HOW?

DO YOU PROVIDE DAILY LESSON PLANS?

No. We have purposely kept from outlining a rigid schedule for you. There is no sacred plan using KONOS except the one that is right for your own family. Your family is unique, created by God as distinct from every other family. Your needs, your temperaments, your schedules are (and should be) different. Does this mean that we are unstructured? No. We believe strongly in having a structure, but that structure should reflect *you*, not *us* or any other curriculum publisher. Please live with the feeling of uncertainty as you map out a structure for your family. Designing your own daily lesson plans may initially frustrate some. You may not feel confident to decide or you may think it requires too much time. Don't worry. You will grow in confidence, as we have, that the decisions you make for how to teach your children are far better than the decisions we would make for you. Families who have used KONOS report:

> *(We love KONOS because it gives) freedom to choose topics and individual activities that best suit each family, yet still study topics.*
>
> J.F.
> Visalia, CA

> *KONOS Curriculum is working so well for us...I love KONOS' freedom with direction.*
>
> C.N.
> Ft. Worth, TX

What we do provide is a unit studies format. Each unit (e.g., Attentiveness) is divided into topics (e.g., Indians). Each topic is divided into weeks of study. We provide suggested Weekly Lesson Plans. You can use them as they are, modify them, or make your own. On the next several pages, we will instruct you on how to set up the best lesson plans for your family. See **HOW DO I PLAN FOR EACH UNIT?** for instructions on how to write daily lesson plans. To help you get started we have Sample Daily Lesson Plans for the first month.

HOW DO I TEACH THE SAME TOPIC TO ALL MY CHILDREN?

Instead of sending each child to a separate corner to study a separate subject, all your children can learn as a family. KONOS is designed to be used with just one child or with several children between the ages of kindergarten and eighth grade. Older children will, of course, gain a greater grasp of the subject matter, but that is okay. This will happen no matter what the content.

There is no topic that ought to be taught at a particular grade level (e.g., dental care in third grade, American history in fourth grade, birds in sixth grade). The only reason that schools sequence subject matter is to be sure that it is covered within the child's education and that it is not unnecessarily repeated. States (and districts within a state) disagree on what is taught in what grade. For example, American history may be taught in fourth, eighth, and eleventh grades in one state and in third, fifth, and ninth in another school. Birds may be taught in second in one district and in fourth in another. Indians may be taught in third in one district and in third and sixth in another. When a child transfers from one district to another or one state to another, he finds that he is repeating or leaving out sections of learning. This demonstrates that there is no absolute grade level for topics. What <u>does</u> need to be taught sequentially, "line upon line, precept upon precept," is reading, language, and math (see Math and Language Checklists). Topics can be learned, however, no matter what the age. There is no typical kindergarten activity. For example, "sculpt a bird" is something that a young child may do quite crudely while an older child may do with more refinement. Look at the following KONOS activities and *try* to put them into a grade level. You will see how ridiculous it would be to assign these activities to a particular grade.

- Ride a horse
- Plant a garden
- Listen to an orchestra
- Pretend to have only one arm
- Dramatize Martha's distractibility

- Make soap
- Visit a machine shop and identify simple machines
- Organize a club and choose officers
- Make Boston baked beans

Younger children will simply do less, while older children will do more. If, for some reason, you want your child to study the same topics as are studied in your local school district that year, refer to your state's scope and sequence and choose the appropriate topics. If not, use our unit study approach. By referring to KONOS' Overview you see that within three volumes all the required material will be covered, although not necessarily in the same sequence as in your school district.

How do we teach all levels? By using the Weekly Lesson Plans, you will see certain reading and writing activities that are for older, middle, and younger children. It is the book list, the writing assignments, and supplemented 3Rs, that keep each of your children at grade level. Start with the books that each child will be reading. Assign writing projects for each. Choose activities for the whole family to do together. Choose activities that will be for just older children to do independently. For example, when studying Ears/Sound/Music in the Attentiveness unit, everyone has something to do. Choose activities for just the younger children. The point is that you know your own child and you know what activities are "right up his alley" as well as those which are too difficult or too easy for him. Remember that younger children will do less, perhaps going to play after a family activity while older children continue to "climb the ladder" doing harder activities. Multi-level teaching is like driving a bus. All the kids start from the same location, but they are let out at different stops along the way.

HOW DO I GET STARTED USING KONOS?

1) Know yourself. Take a weekend away with your spouse and honestly evaluate yourselves and each other. What are you like?

- ambitious vs. steady
- reserved vs. social
- high energy vs. low energy

- high-strung vs. laid-back
- organized vs. serendipidous
- skilled teacher vs. inexperienced teacher

What are your strengths? What are your weaknesses? What rejuvenates you? Everyone is different. For some, it may be very refreshing to teach. For others it may be refreshing to plan and design. For others it may be hiking or socializing or embroidery. I mentioned this at a seminar where one woman admitted that what refreshed her most was cleaning toilets! I am now totally convinced of God's unique design of each of us. It is important to know your temperment, talent, and interests to be prepared for the school year. If you are high-strung, social, and athletic, you will want to be *on the go*. The hardest part of home-schooling will be planning and organizing. By knowing this, you know how to pray for the Lord to *fill in the slots*.

What is your marriage like? Are you struggling? Maybe you need time building your relationship. We have recommended that some couples postpone home-schooling until their relationship is in order. What are the unique characteristics of your marriage? What do you like best about your partnership? How do you complement each other? What things would build your relationship?

What is your lifestyle like right now? Are you busy with a new or demanding job? Are you pregnant? Do you have a baby? Do you have extended family or other help with the children? When we Thaxtons moved to another state, there were months of transition. This obviously affected how we home-schooled. Write a paragraph summary of your current life. What would be best for our whole family this year? Be realistic!

2) Determine mother's and father's roles. In most cases (but not all), the mother is the primary teacher and the father is the primary bread-winner. The father usually acts as the principal or overseer of the children's education, while the mother does the day-to-day teaching. Dads, these are some ways you can help your wife and children to cheerfully succeed at home-schooling:

a) Be a perfect husband (only kidding!!)

Lead, direct, and guard your wife. Do not let her take on too much. Home-schooling is a full-time job. Your wife will need your support more now than any time before. She is taking on a lonely, often misunderstood job, where there is no salary and little affirmation. On the worst of days she will feel like nobody cares what she is doing. She may doubt her own competence and will wonder if it is all worth it. On the best of days she will be excited but weary. She needs you to listen to her (with both eyes focused on her face). Encourage her, guide, and sometimes put your foot down for her. She needs you to help her work through problems, to discipline the children, to help her with the dishes, etc.

Find out how she is feeling. Ask her what you can do to relieve her. A surprise husband/wife weekend get-away (if you plan the details) could be just the thing she needs. Perhaps you could teach some of the school subjects (e.g., P.E., computer, or math) while she has time to herself. You could hire a maid to clean (even once monthly if that is all you can afford). You and the kids could have work days while she has coffee with a friend. The most common complaint we hear among home-schooling moms is "My husband just doesn't seem to realize what all I am doing." Prove that you do. Remember that she is a weaker vessel that you have the privilege of cherishing.

b) Give to your children

First of all, acquaint your children with the Lord. Teach them the Scriptures. Set aside time daily, twice a week, or weekly to share God's Word with them. You may not have a great deal of knowledge, but start with sharing your love for the Lord.

The second best thing you can give your children is love for their mother. Express affection for her. Tell them how wonderful their mother is and how glad you are that you married her. Through your actions, demonstrate how a loving husband cares for his wife. In recent surveys, children say that what they fear most is the break up of their parents and what they want most is for their parents to love each other.

Give your children your time. When fathers say they are working over-time "for the family," it is often untrue. Rather than a new bike, Johnny would rather have Dad spend Saturday helping him fix his old bike. Rather than taking them to a movie, kids would benefit more from doing chores at home *with* you. Don't fool yourself in giving small

27

amounts of "quality time" doing "wonderful planned activities." Children can not be programmed into growing close to their fathers by being given time-slots. It may take a full day of working together in the garage before your son feels comfortable enough to share a problem with you.

Share your skills with them. When you are changing a lightbulb, show your daughter how to do it. When you are mowing the lawn, give your son a chance to try it. When you go to the hardware store, take the kids along and explain how you are deciding which sandpaper to purchase. Talk to them about your work. Share problems with employees and ways to resolve them. Employers can't seem to find reliable employees. If you are a computer expert, share your knowlege about computers. Your job as father is to give them the character and work skills that will make them be successful employees.

Reinforce their learning. Mom is teaching all day. When you come home at night, you can be the reviewer of all they have learned. Ask at the dinner table what they have studied. Let them quiz *you*. Be an audience for their "show and tell." Applaud for the poem they recite. Exclaim over the craft they make. Ask questions about their science experiment. The KONOS way is to involve the whole family in activities together. Please don't feel too foolish dressing up like an Indian and doing a hoop dance. We guarantee that after the initial shock to your system, you'll actually have a good time *and* you will be reinforcing their learning.

3) Know your own children. What are they like? Identify each one's strengths and weaknesses. Think through *what* you need to work on with each child and *how* you will work on it. Every temperament strength has its corresponding weakness. C.J., ambitious, independent, and responsible, can be trusted to follow through on his work. He is bright and interested in learning. "I wish he were *my* son," you may be thinking. But C.J. is the same son who can walk into a room and be oblivious that anyone else is present. He can be insensitive to the needs of others, not even noticing if someone is bleeding. Our work with him is to build awareness and sensitivity. Carson, on the other hand, is very aware of people's feelings. He intuitively knows the right words to use to cheer someone. What a delight! Yet this is the same son who leaves a trail of "I forgots" throughout the house. "I forgot to put back the toothpaste," "I forgot to hang up my clothes," "I forgot to finish dusting." Our job with him is to develop self-discipline. To help identify your child's temperament, we recommend reading Tim LaHaye's <u>Knowing Your Child's Temperament.</u> Also, to identify your child's particular learning style, see Cathy Duffy's "Choose Curriculum to Fit Learning Styles" in <u>The Teaching Home</u>, April-May, 1987.

Know the goals you have for your children. What do you really want for them? If you're not sure, ask God to show you. Be sure both you and your spouse are in agreement about what you really want for them. If you agree with us that KONOS CURRICULUM meets these goals, you are ready to get started.

4) Attend a KONOS Seminar or listen to the tape series HOW TO USE KONOS CURRICULUM. Make contact with a KONOS Counselor if you feel you need further help with getting started. (See **HOW DO I GET HELP WHEN I NEED IT?**)

5) Read through the KONOS Overview in this KONOS COMPASS. You will want to establish a general overall plan for the next several years. Remember that any topic can be learned at any time by any age. You may wish to leave out topics. This depends primarily on the age and experience of your children. If you have older children whom you are removing from school, they may have studied certain topics before. In that case, we would suggest that you cross out the topics you do not want to study and save them for later use with your younger children. If your children are very young, you may want to wait until later years to introduce such topics as the Military or Birth and Human Growth. Below are several plans used by experienced KONOS users. Decide which plan would work best for you.

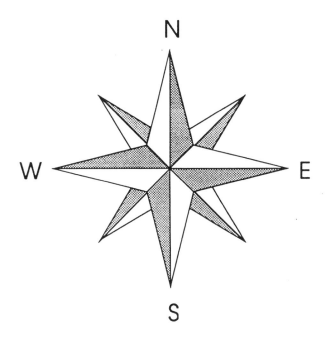

FAMILY A

YEAR 1	Lightly through every unit of Volume I
YEAR 2	Lightly through every unit of Volume III
YEAR 3	Lightly through every unit of Volume II
YEAR 4	More thoroughly through every unit of Volume I
YEAR 5	More thoroughly through every unit of Volume III
YEAR 6	More thoroughly through every unit of Volume II

FAMILY B

YEAR 1	Some units from Volume I
YEAR 2	Some units from Volume II
YEAR 3	Some units from Volume III
YEAR 4	Other units from Volume I
YEAR 5	Other units from Volume II
YEAR 6	Other units from Volume III
YEAR 7	Review of earlier units from all volumes

FAMILY C

YEAR 1	3 units from Volume I
YEAR 2	3 more units from Volume I
YEAR 3	1 unit from Volume I, 2 from Volume II
YEAR 4	3 units from Volume II
YEAR 5	1 unit from Volume II, 2 from Volume III
YEAR 6	3 units from Volume III
YEAR 7	3 units from Volume III

FAMILY D

YEAR 1	First half of Volume I
YEAR 2	Second half of Volume I
YEAR 3	American history units in Volume II
YEAR 4	Other units in Volume II
YEAR 5	First half of Volume III
YEAR 6	Second half of Volume III
YEAR 7	Review some units
YEAR 8	Review other units

FAMILY E

YEAR 1 Some topics within each unit of Volume I

YEAR 2 Other topics within each unit of Volume I

YEAR 3 Some topics within each unit of Volume II

YEAR 4 American history topics from Volume II

YEAR 5 Some topics within each unit of Volume III

YEAR 6 Other topics within each unit of Volume III

YEAR 7 Topics not covered first time around

FAMILY F

(Eliminating topics already covered by older children)

YEAR 1 Some topics from Vol. I

YEAR 2 Some topics from Vol. II

YEAR 3 Some topics from Vol. III

YEAR 4 Volume I for younger children

YEAR 5 Volume II for younger children

YEAR 6 Volume III for younger children

YEAR 7 Topics not previously covered

YEAR 8 Topics not previously covered

FAMILY G

YEAR 1 First half of Volume I

YEAR 2 Second half of Volume I

YEAR 3 First half of Volume II

YEAR 4 Second half of Volume II

YEAR 5 First half of Volume III

YEAR 6 Second half of Volume III

YEAR 7 Repeat first half of Vol. I for younger children

YEAR 8 Repeat second half of Vol. II for younger children

FAMILY H

Each year choose topics from all three of the volumes

HOW DO I SET UP A YEARLY SCHEDULE?

1) Take a few planning days during the summer. If possible, plan a time for husband and wife to get away for a weekend. Before setting up a yearly schedule, take a good look at your year. You may have events (e.g., visits from relatives, harvesting season, an Easter production, a new baby's arrival) during the year that would determine your schedule. Remember that KONOS is designed for families to adapt to their own needs.

2) Determine specific goals for each child. Each year we include a character goal, an academic Goal, physical goals, and some work skills goals. Here are some examples:

> Rhett (age 6)
> Character - orderliness
> Academics - reading
> Physical - gymnastics, soccer, T-ball
> Work Skills - vacuuming, cleaning room
>
> Carson (age 10)
> Character - self-control
> Academics - multiplication/division, language skills
> Physical - soccer
> Work Skills - pet care, child care, assembling Timelines
>
> C.J. (age 13)
> Character - honoring others (sensitivity, etiquette)
> Academics - current affairs
> Physical - basketball
> Work Skills - paid work at apple stand, entering computer data for KONOS

These goals are targets toward which to aim. They are not all that we do with each child, but they are the primary things we want to focus on and make sure we accomplish for the year. We do not ignore the other subjects. We simply concentrate our focus. For one child you might want to concentrate on making learning fun for a change. Perhaps your second child needs to take more responsibility for his own work. Maybe your third child needs to beef up on writing skills. Through observation and standardized testing of academic skills, you can make the best judgment of what your child needs.

3) Pray for your needs. When Carole started writing KONOS she prayed for someone with whom to teach and write. The Lord provided Jessica. Ever since she has warned, "Be careful how you pray; God answers!" Through the years we have prayed for many, many things and watched the Lord's faithfulness. We encourage you to pray together as a family. If the children know where you want to go, they can help you get there. Encourage the kids to pray for each other. One thing we quickly learn as parents is to never underestimate the prayers of a child. When Carson prayed for a "dark blue van with a silver stripe," should we have been surprised that the Lord provided a dark blue van with a silver stripe?

4) Decide if you want to co-op with other families and who they will be this year. You will want to plan your yearly schedule together. (See **HOW DO I CO-OP WITH OTHER FAMILIES?**)

5) Following is a sample yearly schedule using Volume I. Decide which units you want to teach which months.

YEAR 1

Sept.	Attentiveness	General, Ear, Eye, Other Senses
Oct.	Attentiveness	Birds, Predator/Prey
Nov.	Obedience	Bible, Kings and Queens
Dec.	None	
Jan.	Orderliness	Sequencing, Counting, Calendars/Seasons
Feb.	Honor	Countries/Cultures (Japan), Kindness and Etiquette
Mar.	Honor	Tabernacle, Attributes of God, Reverent Behavior/Hymns
Apr.	Trust	General, Sheep/Weaving
May	Patience	All topics, mostly Grain/Bread/Yeast

YEAR 2

Sept.   Attentiveness
        Indians
Oct.   Attentiveness
        Indians, Frontiersmen
Nov,   ~~Nov.~~Honor
        Countries/Cultures (Russia)
Dec.   None
Jan.   Stewardship of the Body
Feb.   Stewardship of Money
          and Possessions
        Stewardship of Time
        Stewardship of Talents
Mar.   Trust
        Flight/Airplanes
Apr.   Obedience
        General, Horses
May   Orderliness
        Plant Classification
        Animal Classification

Contents

Preface
Explanation
Implementation

6) Plan ahead for major field trips.

7) Buy books and supplies. Decide on materials for the 3Rs (reading, writing, and math). Depending on the ages of your children you will need a) phonics and/or spelling programs, b) language arts workbooks which include punctuation, capitalization, and grammar for upper levels, and c) math programs. See **HOW DO I SUPPLEMENT KONOS?** for a list of suggested supplements and where to order them. Your library will be your best and most complete resource. Get to know your library and librarian during the summer. Can you order books through an inter-library loan system? Will your librarian reserve books for you? Are there other resources (e.g., records, films, art works)?

8) Set up work and storage areas. Have your children help in planning and arranging. For example, one child might be in charge of setting up a quiet reading area, while another is in charge of a bulletin board.

9) Design a way to record your children's accomplishments. Here are a few ideas:

   • "Learning Tree" on the wall with "leaves" of accomplishment
   • "Stars" on ceiling with activities accomplished written on them
   • "Bookcase" with titles of books read
   • "Verse Vase" made of a real vase with posterboard "flowers" glued to pipecleaner "stems" with verses memorizede "Art Gallery" clothesline with works of art attached with clothespins
   • "Rhett's Rocket Reading Club" poster on which he drew a rocket ship and stuck star stickers for every ten pages read

10) Plan a reward system. Even older children enjoy recognition and rewards for what they have accomplished. Through the years we have used stickers, baseball cards, stamps for a stamp collection, hair barettes and ribbons, special nutritional treats, more free play, special dates with Dad, overnights with friends, rental of videos, etc., to reward our children. We realize they should (when completely sanctified) do everything without thought of reward. Yet, we agree with James Dobson that not many adults would go to work unless they were paid a salary.

HOW DO I SET UP A WEEKLY SCHEDULE?

In addition to your KONOS activities, be sure to include the following unless you have incorporated them into your unit studies.

   • Parents' time with the Lord
   • Individual time with each child
   • Unit studies (KONOS)
   • Co-oping with other families
   • Music, art, or other lessons
   • Planning for the following week
   • Review (wrap-up of what has been learned that week)

   • Parents' rest and fun
   • 3 Rs (reading, writing, math)
   • Family times
   • Sports or other exercise
   • Weekly chores
   • Worship
   • Service to others (e.g. demonstrating something learned at a nursing home)

You can probably guess which ones are most likely to be eliminated—the first two. Please take care of yourself. You deserve it and your kids need it. Here are sample weekly schedules of families using KONOS.

	Family A	Family B	Family C
SUNDAY	Worship Service to others	Worship Bible study Rest	Worship R & R
MONDAY	Bible KONOS	3Rs KONOS	Bible Spelling/Language KONOS Boy Scouts
TUESDAY	Bible 3Rs Music lessons	3Rs KONOS Gymnastics	Bible Math KONOS
WEDNESDAY	Bible KONOS CO-OP Soccer	3Rs KONOS	Bible Spelling/Language KONOS Sports
THURSDAY	Bible 3Rs Parents' date night	3Rs KONOS Gymnastics Weekly planning	Bible Math KONOS Art class Weekly planning
FRIDAY	Bible KONOS review 3Rs review Family night	3Rs KONOS Review	Bible 3Rs review KONOS review Family fun
SATURDAY	Soccer Weekly planning Fun	Chores Family fun	Chores Sports

You can see that to balance KONOS with the 3Rs you can either do the basic skills every day along with KONOS or do basic skills a few days a week with "homework" throughout the week and KONOS on the other days. The important thing to keep in mind is the balance. If you have had kids sitting at desks doing seatwork for years, you are better off putting weight on the side of KONOS. If you have been burning yourself out with exciting activities, it is best to put weight on the side of the 3Rs. The ideal is a balance between the two. Don't lose sight, however, that when doing KONOS you *are* doing academics. Just because most of the activities are *fun* does not mean that they are less *academic*. Quite the contrary!

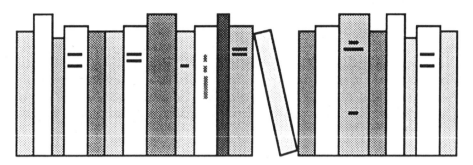

HOW DO I SET UP A DAILY SCHEDULE?

Parents often ask how much time to spend on "school." Please keep in mind that all of life is learning and it is sometimes difficult to divide what is educational and what is not. For the most part, we recommend concentrating on formal instruction during the mornings and saving special projects and independent "homework" for the afternoons. Pre-schoolers and kindergarteners should have one-half hour segments of work with a physical break in between. Most first and second-graders can handle an hour at a time. Older children can begin planning their own schedules. A few sample daily schedules follow:

Family A has one child, age 8.	Family B has two children, ages 9 and 6.	Family C has 4 children, ages 10, 8, 5 and 4.
6:30 - 7:30 Exercise; Breakfast; Grooming	6:30 Exercise; Breakfast; Chores; Parents' prayer	5:45 - 6:15 Mom walks
7:30 - 8:00 Morning chores (make beds, wash dishes, tidy up); Practice instrument	8:00 Family time (Bible, character examples, discussion of character trait, prayer)	6:15 - 7:00 Shower, dress, pick up rooms; Mom showers and has quiet time
8:00 - 8:30 Bible; Character objectives; Prayer	8:30 KONOS activities or 3Rs	7:00 - 7:45 Breakfast; Family time (Bible, character discussion, prayer)
8:30 - 9:30 Reading skills (phonics and spelling)	10:30 Break	7:45 - 8:30 Chores (cleaning, sort laundry, pets)
9:30 - 10:30 Math skills	11:00 KONOS activities or 3Rs	8:30 - 9:00 Handwriting, phonics and spelling (youngers); Spelling and language (olders)
10:30 - 11:00 Calisthenics, game, sport	12:00 Lunch; Chores (Cleaning, laundry, baking, yardwork)	9:00 - 9:30 Math
11:00 - 12:00 KONOS activities	1:30 Special projects and "homework" (language and math workbooks and KONOS reading)	9:30 - 10:30 KONOS activities
12:00 - 1:30 Lunch and discussion; Weekly chores (cleaning, laundry)	3:00 (or whenever work is done); Free play; Sports; Music lessons	10:30 - 11:00 Exercise, sport, snack
1:30 - 3:00 KONOS activities	5:00 Set table, help prepare dinner	11:00 - 12:30 KONOS activities
3:00 - 5:00 Free time	6:00 Dinner; Time with Dad	12:30 - 1:30 Lunch and break
5:00 - 5:30 Pick up, set table	7:00 Bath; Family reading; Crafts	1:30 - 3:00+ Writing with Mom's assistance; Independent writing; Language workbooks; Math practice; Reading; Chores (fold laundry, gather firewood, clean)
5:30 - 6:00 Time with Dad		3:00+ - 5:30 Free time
6:00 - 6:30 Dinner		5:30 - 6:00 Help prepare dinner, set table
6:30 - 7:00 Baths		6:00 - 7:00 Dinner and discussion
7:00 - 8:00 Family reading		7:00 - 9:00 Boy Scouts, Youth Alive, sports practice and/or family reading (Friday night friends, games, and/or KONOS presentation)

FAMILY D has four children, ages 13, 9, 6, and 6 months. They also have a live-in maid who helps with domestic work and watches the baby during school time.

	MONDAY	TUESDAY	WEDNESDAY	THURSDAY	FRIDAY
6:00 - 6:20	Dress and clean room	Dress and clean room	Dress and clean room	Dress and clean room	Dress and clean room
6:20 - 7:00	Exercise on tape while Mom prays and walks	Exercise on tape while Mom prays and walks; breakfast	Exercise on tape while Mom prays and walks	Exercise on tape while Mom prays and walks; breakfast	Exercise on tape while Mom prays and walks; breakfast
7:00 - 8:00	Eat breakfast & talk; Mom bathes and feeds baby	Bible & hymns w/ Dad; Mom bathes & feeds baby	Eat breakfast; Mom bathes & feeds baby	Bible & hymns w/ Dad; Mom bathes & feeds baby	Bible & hymns w/ Dad; Mom bathes & feeds baby
8:00 - 8:45	Oldest types; Mom helps youngers with phonics	Oldest types; Mom helps youngers with phonics	Oldest types; Mom helps youngers with phonics	Oldest types; Mom helps youngers with phonics	Oldest types; Mom helps youngers with phonics
8:45 - 9:15	Olders do language; Mom reads to youngest	Youngest does spelling; Mom helps olders w/ language	KONOS Co-op	Youngest does spelling; Mom helps olders w/ language	Olders do language; Mom reads to youngest
9:15 - 10:00	Oldest writes letters; middle reads; Mom helps youngest with spelling	Youngest does spelling; Mom helps olders w/ language	KONOS Co-op	Youngest does spelling; Mom helps olders w/ language	Oldest writes letters; middle reads; Mom helps youngest with spelling
10:00 - 10:30	Sports	Sports	KONOS Co-op	Sports	Sports
10:30 - 11:30	KONOS	KONOS	KONOS Co-op	KONOS	KONOS
11:30 - 12:30	Olders do math; Mom does math with youngest	Olders do math; Mom does math with youngest	KONOS Co-op	Olders do math; Mom does math with youngest	KONOS art projects
12:30 - 1:00	Lunch and Spanish	Lunch and Spanish	KONOS Co-op	Lunch and Spanish	Lunch and Spanish.
1:00 - 1:30	BREAK	BREAK	KONOS Co-op	BREAK	BREAK
1:30 - 4:00	Reading, violin, KONOS projects	Reading, violin, KONOS projects	KONOS Co-op Free play	Reading, violin, KONOS projects	Reading, violin, KONOS projects
5:45 - 6:15	Dinner	Dinner	Dinner	Dinner	Dinner
6:30 - 8:00	Football practice	Boy Scouts	Family activities	Football practice	Family activities
8:30 - 9:00	Literature sometimes	Literature sometimes	Literature sometimes	Literature sometimes	Literature sometimes
9:00 - 9:30	Bath and bed	Bath and bed	Bath and bed	Bath and bed	Bath and bed

But remember that just because you have a schedule does not mean that every day is going to flow smoothly. Take yesterday, for example:

6:00	Turn over and hit the snooze alarm
6:10	Turn over and hit the snooze alarm
6:20	Turn over and hit the snooze alarm
6:30	Turn over and hit the snooze alarm
6:40	Turn over and hit the snooze alarm
6:40	Get up and throw clothes on
6:45	Yell at everybody to get out of bed
6:50	Yell again
6:55	Yell again louder
7:00	Burn toast while toddler dumps box of oatmeal on the floor
7:05	Clean oatmeal off the floor while toddler helps by pouring water on it
7:10	Clean up oatmeal "help"
7:15	Scrape toast
7:20	Call everyone for breakfast
	Dad says grace and Mom prays _for_ grace
7:25	Give the lecture about appreciating the food that is set before you
7:30	Clean up spilt milk
7:35	Reprimand six-year-old for his toast-crust-in-milk buoyancy experiment
7:40	Reprimand everybody else "just because"
7:45	Have family Bible study about a "peaceable and quiet spirit"
8:40	Apologize for starting the day off on the wrong foot
8:45	Give list of chores to everyone
8:50	Retrieve four-year-old's list from the toilet
8:55	Settle the argument about whose dirty sock is on the floor
9:00	Rejoice in all things
9:05	Comfort oldest son who thinks he has too much to do
9:10	Give oldest son more to do
9:15	Comfort youngest son who got yelled at by oldest son
9:25	Comfort self by remembering you _could_ send them all off to school
9:30	Start school
9:35	Answer phone call from a new home-schooling mom who wants to know how I do it!

And that was just the beginning! Seriously, there will always be interruptions and afflictions in this world, home-schooling or not. *But* if your day is more often like the above, something is wrong. This should not be the norm for a home-schooling family. Perhaps you are trying to do too much. Ask your husband. Perhaps you are burning out by not having a balanced life with rest and recreation as a part of life. Perhaps you need to go to bed earlier or start your school day later. Whatever it takes, do it. A routine makes life run more smoothly, helps children feel more secure, and helps mother feel satisfied with taking dominion over her household. How rigid your schedule is depends upon what you and your family are like. Are you a mom that is always reading *"how to get more organized"* books? Perhaps you do need to get better control over your life. Do you always *"race"* through the day with no *"breathing space?"* Perhaps you need to be less rigid and flex more.

How many children do you have, what are they like, and how old are they? If you have young children, you <u>have</u> to flex whether you want to or not. You cannot control when a child is going to ask, "Are you going to die?," "How are babies made?," "Where is Jesus?" You cannot control when a child is going to fall out of a chair or when a baby is going to feel colicky. As your children grow and as your family grows, you will find the increasing need to be organized. If not, your total waking time will be taken up trying to remember if you have clean diapers, if the kids have had dental check-ups, if your first-grader has learned to read, if your dog has had rabies shots, if your fourth-grader can divide, if you paid the telephone bill, if the Boy Scout dues are paid, if you've returned library books on time, if you have something prepared for dinner, and if you have left a kid behind at Del Taco (as I once did!). If you have active, difficult children, you will need to impose more order for them and yet flex on the things that don't matter as much. With a hyperactive son, we had to regiment a consistent routine to teach self-control, but we ignored the condition of the backyard since we needed an area to "let him loose."

The KONOS way is individualized. We want you to minister to your own families consistent with the way God made each of you. We do encourage you to organize your time *in order to* love your family. If, at any time, the order infringes on that love, please reconsider your schedule. Keep your perspective. Remember that the *most* important question is "Am I loving the Lord and am I loving my family?"

I Corinthians 13 for Home-Schooling Moms*

Though I teach with the very best skills,
But do not have love,
I am just drawing attention to myself.
And if I have experience, and knowledge of all the best techniques,
*   and test results proving my effectiveness*
But do not have love,
I am wasting my time.
And if I work hard, sacrificing all my money, my time, and my energy
But do not have love,
It adds up to nothing.

The loving teacher is patient with her children, allowing them to learn
*   according to their God-given temperaments and developmental rates.*
She is kind, treating her children respectfully.
She does not compare herself with others.
She does not brag about her accomplishments, and is not smug
*   about teaching her own children.*
She does not try to be like anyone else, but acts appropriate to the way
*   God made her.*
She is not irritable and pushy and insistent upon making her children
*   fit into her lesson plans.*
She is more concerned with promoting truth and beauty than
*   with criticizing those who don't.*
She perseveres in developing her own character, believing that God's ways
*   are always best. She is not a quitter.*
Love never fails.

If there are creative ideas, they will be replaced.
If there are great curricula, they will be superseded.
If there are effective techniques, they will be improved.
All that we know now is only a part.
Only later will God reveal education at its best.
When I was a child, I had unrealistic expectations.
As an adult, I know better.
Now abideth faith, hope, and love.
But the greatest of these is love.

*And Dads

HOW DO I PLAN EACH UNIT?

1) Refer back to your yearly plan to determine how much time you plan to spend on the unit. Decide the amount of time you want to spend on each topic. Within each unit we have included weekly lesson plans. For example for Horses in the Obedience unit, we have divided the topic into four weeks:

Week 1: General information
Breeds
Points and anatomy
Sketching

Week 2: Tack
Horse care
Riding

Week 3: Horse events (racing, showing, dressage, jumping)

Week 4: Cowboys
Frederic Remington
Painting horses

You can, of course, make the unit longer or shorter as you desire.

2) Collect resources.

Check to see what books you have in your home (e.g., King of the Wind or Black Beauty. Go to your local library and check out the books you will need (books for parent reference, about two books for each child's reading and/or writing skills, books for older children to read to younger children or parents to read to everyone). Look for specific books that have an asterisk (*) and order them through inter-library loan if necessary. The card catalogue number is listed at the beginning of the Resource List. Go to that section of the library and look for other or additional books. Check your library's card catalogue for additional books under that topic. A "J" listing indicates that it is a juvenile fictional book. Look for it by author's name. Use these books for family reading or independent reading for older children. "ER" books are easy readers for your beginning reader. "E" books are picture books with or without words for you to read to your younger children. Choose a few books for reference and two books for each child. Also check out films, cassettes, records, statues, paintings, and other resources from your library.

3) Make lesson plans.

a) Divide the unit into weekly lesson plans. Use the ones we have provided or write your own. On the KONOS Weekly Lesson Plans, you see "Theme." This is the overall category of what will be studied that week. "Bible" refers to the Bible verses, stories, and biblical characters that will be studied that week. "Audio-visual Resources" refers to films, tapes, records, paintings, videos, and other audio-visuals. "Books" are divided into "older," "middle," and "younger." Each level has a writing assignment as indicated by "Writing." "Family Activities" are suggested activities to do as a family. "Co-op Activities" are those activities to do within your co-op.

b) Keep a balance. Many home-school beginners make the mistake of "slipping off the see-saw." Parents may be reacting *against* something in their own or their children's previous education, and swing the pendulum too far, thus "throwing the baby out with the bathwater." Often parents concentrate either too much on 3R skill-building or try too hard to "make all learning fun." Some are so over-scheduled and intensely concentrated that they and their children quickly become weary; others are too laid-back, afraid of demanding too much from their children. Many beginners spend all their time with their children, focusing too much individual attention on each child rather than allowing some room to develop independence and self-responsibility. Some have the mistaken notion that if we take off the restraints, children will adequately teach themselves. Most experienced home-schoolers see the value of both/and rather than either/or. Make a rough draft of the Bible, audio-visual resources, books, writing projects, and activities you will do for each week of the unit. Then ask yourself the following questions:

- *Is there a balance between reading/writing (seatwork) and doing (experiential activities)?*

- *Is there a balance between talking to my children (telling) and letting them discover things on their own (discovery)?*

- *Is there a balance between group activity (family or co-op) and individual attention?*

- *Is there a balance between supervised work and independent work?*

- *Is there a balance between intense, concentrated focus and easy, less intense work?*

- *Is there a balance between building skills in the 3Rs and involvement in unit studies (KONOS)?*

- *Is there a balance between scheduled time and free time?*

- *Is there a balance between academics and practical living skills?*

c) Plan for special events like field trips or presentations. When planning a field trip, be sure to call in advance about date, hours, cost, and directions. If possible, speak directly to the person who will be your guide. Tell him/her the nature of what you are studying and what you hope the children will accomplish through the field trip. Be sure to note on your calendar who will write a thank you note.

d) Write out your week's schedule. Refer back to your weekly schedule. You may want to photocopy a weekly schedule with the fixed events (e.g., laundry, soccer, piano lessons) on it. See the following lesson plan guides that some KONOS families have used. There is a blank weekly calendar for you to make your own.

LESSON PLAN GUIDE

Family A

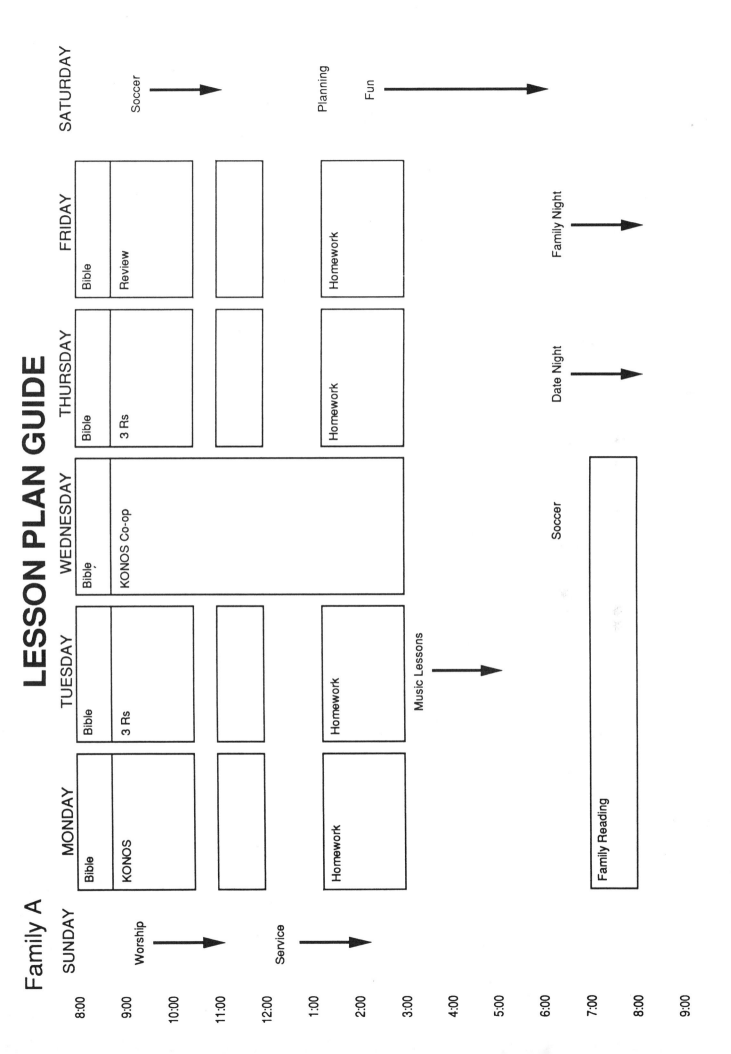

	SUNDAY	MONDAY	TUESDAY	WEDNESDAY	THURSDAY	FRIDAY	SATURDAY
8:00		Bible	Bible	Bible	Bible	Bible	
9:00	Worship →	KONOS	3 Rs	KONOS Co-op	3 Rs	Review	Soccer →
10:00							
11:00							
12:00	Service →						Planning
1:00		Homework	Homework		Homework	Homework	Fun →
2:00			Homework				
3:00			Music Lessons →				
4:00							
5:00							
6:00				Soccer			
7:00		Family Reading					
8:00					Date Night →	Family Night →	
9:00							

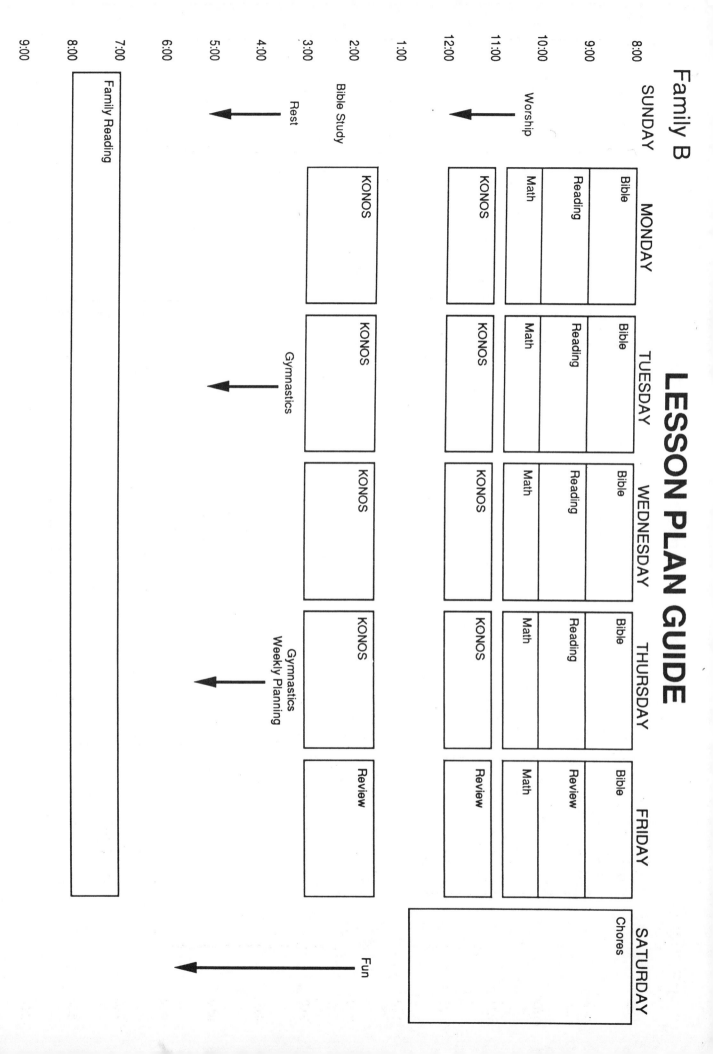

Family B

LESSON PLAN GUIDE

	SUNDAY	MONDAY	TUESDAY	WEDNESDAY	THURSDAY	FRIDAY	SATURDAY
8:00							
9:00		Bible	Bible	Bible	Bible	Bible	
10:00		Reading	Reading	Reading	Reading	Review	
11:00	Worship	Math	Math	Math	Math	Math	
12:00		KONOS	KONOS	KONOS	KONOS	Review	
1:00	←						
2:00	Bible Study	KONOS	KONOS	KONOS	KONOS	Review	Chores
3:00							
4:00	Rest		Gymnastics		Gymnastics Weekly Planning		
5:00	←		←		←		
6:00							Fun
7:00							←
8:00	Family Reading						
9:00							

LESSON PLAN GUIDE

Family C

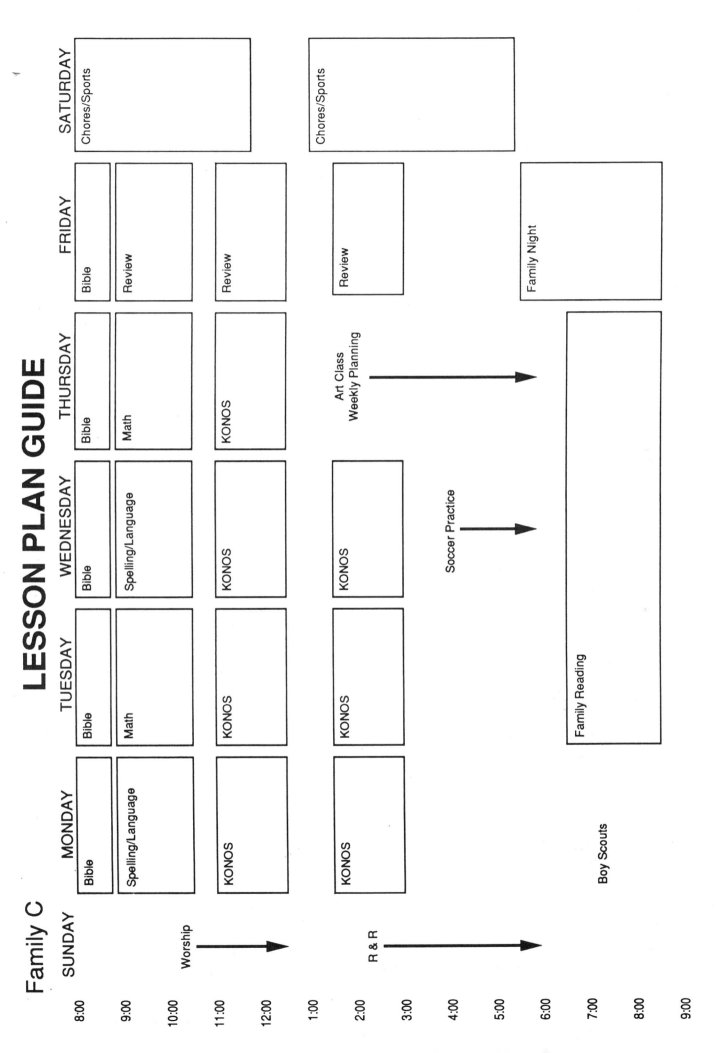

	SUNDAY	MONDAY	TUESDAY	WEDNESDAY	THURSDAY	FRIDAY	SATURDAY
8:00		Bible	Bible	Bible	Bible	Bible	Chores/Sports
9:00	Worship →	Spelling/Language	Math	Spelling/Language	Math	Review	
10:00							
11:00		KONOS	KONOS	KONOS	KONOS	Review	
12:00							
1:00	R & R →	KONOS	KONOS	KONOS		Review	Chores/Sports
2:00					Art Class Weekly Planning →		
3:00				Soccer Practice →			
4:00							
5:00			Family Reading			Family Night	
6:00							
7:00		Boy Scouts					
8:00							
9:00							

LESSON PLAN GUIDE

Family D

* Mom involved

Time	SUNDAY	MONDAY	TUESDAY	WEDNESDAY	THURSDAY	FRIDAY	SATURDAY
7:00							
8:00		Bible	Bible	Bible	Bible	Bible	
9:00		Typing / L.A. / Letter Writing	Typing / L.A.*	Typing	Typing / L.A.*	Typing / Writing / L.A.	
10:00		Phonics* / L.A. / Reading	Phonics* / L.A.*	Phonics*	Phonics* / L.A.*	Phonics* / L.A. / Reading	
11:00	Worship →	Phonics* / Reading / Spelling*	Phonics* / Spelling	Phonics*	Phonics* / Spelling	Phonics* / Reading / Spelling*	
12:00		KONOS: Math / Math / Math*	KONOS: Math / Math / Math*	KONOS Co-op	KONOS: Math / Math / Math*		
1:00	Rest & Plan →						
2:00		Homework	Homework		Review		
3:00					Art Project		
4:00					Homework		
5:00					Service/Violin Lessons		
6:00							
7:00		Boy Scouts		Football	Football		
8:00							
9:00		Literature					Sports →

	SUNDAY	MONDAY	TUESDAY	WEDNESDAY	THURSDAY	FRIDAY	SATURDAY
6:00							
7:00							
8:00							
9:00							
10:00							
11:00							
12:00							
1:00							
2:00							
3:00							
4:00							
5:00							
6:00							
7:00							
8:00							
9:00							
10:00							

e) Choose the books that will provide the content for your week of study. Choose two books for each child at his/her reading level.

f) Decide on a writing project for each child (e.g., report, story, poem).

g) Write down the activities you would like to do each day. If you have a co-op, of course you will do the group activities during those days. On a typical KONOS Day, we spend the first hour and a half giving information, a half hour doing something physical, an hour and a half doing activities, an hour eating lunch and playing, another hour and half doing activities, and a half-hour wrapping up. The first hour and a half segment is primarily talking and showing. In the horse unit, for example, we would show pictures of horses, point out the breeds, and discuss how they compare and contrast. We might tell stories about famous horses and their breeds. We would identify markings on horses and learn their names. We would show a picture of a horse and write the names of the points on the picture. During the half-hour physical break, we would play horseshoes. An hour and a half segment of activities follows the break. During this time we label our own horse picture, play pin the point on the horse, and see actual horses (or a video of horses) to identify breeds, markings, and points. After lunch, we sketch horses, talking about the breeds, markings, and points as we sketch. The last half hour we let the kids quiz each other on the information they have learned, taking turns with a pointer and horse pictures.

h) Plug in your supplements (3Rs). When possible, adapt your children's reading and language skills to correspond to the KONOS topic. (Please refer to **HOW DO I SUPPLEMENT KONOS?** for information on how to do this.)

To get you started, we have written out one month's worth of detailed, daily lesson plans. If this intimidates you, close the book and start with your own plan.

Sample Daily Lesson Plans
One Month of Attentiveness Unit

This particular family has an eight year-old daughter and an eleven-year-old daughter. Every day they followed the same basic plan:

6:30	-	7:30	Exercise, Breakfast, Grooming
7:30	-	8:00	Morning Chores
8:00	-	8:30	Bible, Character, Prayer
8:30	-	9:30	Reading and Spelling
9:30	-	10:30	Math
10:30	-	11:00	Calisthenics, Games
11:00	-	12:00	KONOS
12:00	-	1:30	Lunch and Weekly Chores
1:30	-	3:00	KONOS
3:00	-	5:00	Free Play
5:00	-	5:30	Pick Up, Set Table
5:30	-	6:30	Dinner, Time with Dad
6:30	-	7:00	Baths
7:00	-	8:00	Family Reading and Social Activities

Since KONOS activities were done daily from 8:00 to 8:30 during Bible and Character time, and from 11:00 to 12:00 and 1:30 to 3:00, each day is divided into these time slots.

WEEK 1 - GENERAL ATTENTIVENESS

Monday

8:00 - 8:30   Define attentiveness.
Activity w.
Why is it important? How were we created so that we can be attentive?
Read I Sam. 3:1-14.
Activity a.
Put Samuel on Timeline. Pray.

11:00 - 12:00   Activities c, d.
Discuss how one feels when it doesn't appear that the other person
is listening. Write a story (continue for homework).

1:30 - 3:00   Activities b, f, g, h.

Tuesday

8:00 - 8:30   Activity a.
Review the story of Samuel. Dramatize it. Pray.

11:00 - 12:00   Activities i, k.

1:30 - 3:00   Activity l (watch TV with volume turned off).
Activities m, n, j.

Wednesday

8:00 - 8:30   Read Mark 10:13-16.
Why did Jesus pay attention to little children?
Was Jesus once a child? What was He like?
How do you feel knowing that Jesus pays attention to you? Pray.

11:00 - 12:00   Activity o.
Activity p (use Repeat from Radio Shack; graph results to show how practice improves performance).

1:30 - 3:00   Activity q (walk around a silent route using only signs for direction).
Activity s (tell and write a few words from different languages; see if the girls can
identify the language after hearing them a second time).

Thursday

8:00 - 8:30   Activity e.
Discuss how Jesus always paid attention to His Father. Find examples from Jesus'
life when He paid attention (e.g., the temptations, Gethsemane). Pray.

11:00 - 12:00   Activities t, u.

1:30 - 3:00   Activity y.
Activity z (clip out ads from magazines; discuss if each is convincing and why).
Activity aa (while paying attention and not paying attention).

Friday

8:00 - 8:30   Read Luke 10:38-42. Activity bb.
Dramatize it. How does this compare to modern-day life? Pray.

11:00 - 12:00   Activity cc (make list of improvements to be made). Start changes.

1:30 - 3:00   Decide on a person (e.g., family member) to mimic. Study his speech, body movements, and characteristic behaviors. Collect props that are characteristic. Write a
short script. Dramatize. Have the rest of the family guess who it is. Put on a
show for Dad when he gets home.

WEEK 2 - EARS/SOUND/MUSIC

Monday (Ear)

8:00 - 8:30	Read and memorize Prov. 20:12. Why did God give us ears?
11:00 - 12:00	Read The Story of Your Ears. Activity b (draw and label ear parts). Activity c (set up ear canal).
1:30 - 3:00	Activities g, k, m (bb if time allows). Activity o (start reading aloud The Helen Keller Story; continue during family reading time during the week).

Tuesday (Deafness)

8:00 - 8:30	Find and read Is. 55:3. Discuss. Why does God allow deafness? Why isn't this world perfect? Pray.
11:00 - 12:00	Activities l, p.
1:30 - 3:00	Continue activity p.

Wednesday (Sound - Vibrations)

8:00 - 8:30	Read Is. 55:3 and contrast with Gen. 3:1-7. What "words" do we hear today that distract us from the truth? Pray.
11:00 - 12:00	Activity x during Calisthenics. Activities e, f, h, i.
1:30 - 3:00	Activities aa, cc, dd, ff, gg. Review. Watch video of Alexander Graham Bell in the evening.

Thursday (Sound - Pitch, Volume, Speed)

8:00 - 8:30	Find and read Prov. 25:12. What is a "wise reprove?" Give examples of times you have received a "wise reprove." What could happen if you didn't listen? Draw a cartoon to depict this Proverb. Pray.
11:00 - 12:00	Activities bbb, iii, kkk, lll.
1:30 - 3:00	Activities www, bbbb, hhhh, iiii. "Show and Tell" for Dad in the evening.

Friday (Music - Orchestra)

8:00 - 8:30	Find and read Ps. 150. Discuss the use of instruments in worship. Which ones are most appropriate? Why? Sing and play instruments in worship.
11:00 - 12:00	Activities eee (watch video), fff.
1:30 - 3:00	Activity ggg. Review sound and music. Attend live orchestra with Dad in the evening.

WEEK 3 - EYES/SEEING

Monday (Eye)

8:00 - 8:30	Find and read Matt. 13:16-17. Explain and discuss.
	How is it possible to have eyes but not see and ears but not hear?
	Has this ever happened to you? Give examples.
	What can you do to insure that you will hear what God speaks and see what God has written?
	Pray.
11:00 - 12:00	Read <u>Blood and Guts</u> (section on the eye).
	Activity c (draw and label eye parts).
1:30 - 3:00	Activity d (dissect cow's eye).
	Activities g, h (if time allows).
	Start a biography of Louis Braille during Family Reading; finish during the week.

Tuesday (Eyesight)

8:00 - 8:30	Find and read Matt. 6:22.
	Discuss the eye as the lamp of the body.
	How does what we see affect the rest of us?
	Give examples (e.g., TV, videos, pornography, fashion magazines).
	Pray.
11:00 - 12:00	Activities k, i, n, r.
1:30 - 3:00	Field trip (activity l).
	Interview eye doctor. Investigate equipment.
	Go to optician (eye glass store).
	Observe bifocals, contact lenses, safety lenses, etc.

Wednesday (Camera)

8:00 - 8:30	Find and read Acts 9 (activity jj). Dramatize.
	Discuss how God used Paul's eyes to get his attention.
	Contrast Paul before and after his blindness. Pray.
11:00 - 12:00	Activity f.
	Activity e or ll (finish for homework).
1:30 - 3:00	Take pictures with a camera. Get photos developed at a one-hour processing store. Critique the photos.

Thursday (Magnification)

8:00 - 8:30	Find, read, and discuss Luke 6:41 (activity a).
	Pray.
11:00 - 12:00	Activity z.
	Use a magnifying glass and then a microscope to observe household objects (e.g., paper, hair, rubber band, lint).
1:30 - 3:00	Activities ff, pp.

Friday (Blindness)

8:00 - 8:30	Read John 9 (activity hh). Dramatize.
	Express thanks to God for our eyesight. Pray.
11:00 - 12:00	Activities dd, s.
1:30 - 3:00	Review.
	Read papers written.
	Summarize the life of Louis Braille.
	Add Braille to the Timeline.

WEEK 4 - OTHER SENSES

Monday (Touch)

8:00 - 8:30   Review Bible verses from last week.
Discuss why God gave us our senses and possible consequences of not having these senses.
Pray.

11:00 - 12:00   Activities f, c, b, e.

1:30 - 3:00   Activities d, h.
Assign activities i or j for homework.

Tuesday (Smell)

8:00 - 8:30   Read Gen. 1:31. God said that everything He made was good, but a nose? How is a nose good?
List benefits of having a nose.
Thank God for our noses.
Pray.

11:00 - 12:00   Read Blood and Guts (section on the nose).
Activities k, o, bb.

1:30 - 3:00   Go to the library. Research bloodhounds (activity l) and other animals with a highly developed sense of smell.
Write a description of one animal.
Find an animal story to read during Family Reading.

Wednesday (Taste)

8:00 - 8:30   Find and read Ps. 34:8. What does it mean to "taste Jesus?"
Give examples to the kids about times when we have "tasted" Jesus (i.e., let God be good in our lives) and what He did.
Pray.

11:00 - 12:00   Read Blood and Guts (section on tongue).
Activities m, r, p, n.

1:30 - 3:00   Field trip (activity aa). Find unusual foods at the supermarket. Prepare an exotic dinner.

Thursday (Combination of all senses)

8:00 - 8:30   Find and read Luke 24:36-44.
Explain how God uses our senses to make Himself known (e.g., seeing the written Word, seeing Jesus after He rose from the dead, hearing Israel's history).
Pray.

11:00 - 12:00   Activities u, v.

1:30 - 3:00   Activities y, z, cc.

Friday (Review of all senses)

8:00 - 8:30   Find and read John 20:27.
Does Jesus want us to doubt Him? Does He want us to be honest with Him? How does He answer our questions and doubts? (Instruct how God deals with each of us individually.)
Pray, being honest about our questions and doubts.

11:00 - 12:00   Review all the senses.
Look at family photo albums or movies. Which senses were developed first? How did they progress? Which senses deteriorate with age?

1:30 - 3:00   Visit a nursing home. Share artwork, papers written, etc. Bring a small gift for each person visited.

HOW DO I SUPPLEMENT KONOS?

Whenever possible, we have incorporated reading, writing, and math skills within the topic we are studying. For example, when studying Systems of the Body in the Cooperation unit, we read biographies of famous biologists and physicians (reading), we wrote a novel about a trip through the human body (language), and we measured and did ratios of body parts (math). When possible, we combine KONOS topics with the language arts program. For example, when our oldest was studying the proper placement of commas, we had him discover how Tolkien used commas in The Hobbit in the Books topic of the Honesty unit. Since he was assigned to write a fictional story, we concentrated on the correct placement of commas in his writing. When our middle-level son was studying the correct use of quotation marks, he wrote a dialogue between Columbus and his colleagues arguing about whether the earth was round or flat. This was during the Explorers/Navigation/Sailing topic of the Inquisitiveness unit.

While KONOS does provide all the necessary skill-building in science, social studies, art, music, literature, and health and safety, it is not, however, a complete curriculum in reading (phonics/reading comprehension/spelling), language (capitalization/punctuation/language usage), and math. Supplements to KONOS are very important. While KONOS allows you to teach your children the way they learn best and to create a love of learning, the supplements provide particular reading, language, and math skills. These are the skills that are traditionally measured by standardized tests. Standardized tests are usually divided into a verbal section (reading comprehension, grammar usage, spelling, vocabulary) and non-verbal section (math and sometimes map skills). The supplements listed below are recommended to create a proficiency in these areas.

There are many supplements available. We, like most home-schoolers, have used an array of workbooks and programs. The supplements listed are merely those that worked best for us, and we feel that they are worthy of your examining. This is not an exhaustive or authoritative list. As new products are published or made known to us, we may revise this list. We are sharing from our own experiences using our own criteria. You, like us, need to establish your own criteria and make your own judgments. You also need to recognize special needs of each of your children and then purchase programs that meet each child's needs. For instance, within our two families, we have one child with poor visual memory and another with certain other learning problems. While having successfully used many of the resources listed below, these children have also needed more finely tailored programs to teach to their weaknesses. We cannot begin to advise in those areas on this simple list.

These are the criteria we used to choose each book:

- effectiveness in teaching the skill
- ease of use
- low cost.

The workbooks are published by both Christian and non-Christian publishers; some non-Christian publishers are, in our opinion, more effective and efficient in teaching particular skills. There are also many excellent programs that cost hundreds of dollars, yet we have chosen ones as effective that cost less.

In using any workbooks, we offer four rules of caution:

1) DO NOT push your child into workbooks. Make sure he is ready and make sure the workbook content is on his *ability* level not just his *grade* level. What we show on our chart is the *earliest* we would do any workbooks. If your child is not ready, don't start.

2) DO NOT feel compelled to work every page or *"finish"* each book. If your child uses periods appropriately, then skip the six pages on periods. Or you may use one workbook for more than one year. Make the workbooks fit your child's needs rather than making your child fit the workbooks.

3) DO NOT think you must spend time in each workbook each day. Stagger or rotate workbooks. Depending on each child's level, we do workbooks from one to three hours on the days chosen for the 3Rs. (See **HOW DO I SET UP A WEEKLY SCHEDULE?**)

4) DO NOT feel compelled in the least to use all the workbooks listed. Over the years, we have used very few of the reading comprehension and vocabulary books, since doing KONOS activities and reading related library books has given our boys excellent vocabularies and reading comprehension skills without using workbooks to focus on these skills. However, these books can be a means of checking or reinforcing these skills, if you desire. Use workbooks to fill in the gaps and to reinforce what your child needs.

Suggested Supplements

PRE-PHONICS

Alphabet Activities by Jill M. Condron
    Grade: P-K (in one book)
    Cost: $9.95
    Order: Constructive Playthings
                1227 East 119th Street
                Grandview, MO 64030
                1-800-255-6124

A wonderful book with three pages of easy activities (art, math, science, cooking, physical exercise, and games) for each letter of the alphabet.

PHONICS

The Writing Road to Reading by Romalda Bishop Spaulding
    Grade: K-7 (in one book)
    Cost: $15.00; Teacher's Edition $38.50
    Order: Riggs Institute
                4185 S.W. 102nd Ave.
                Beaverton, OR 97005
                (503) 646-9459 (Let it ring)

This phonics program has 70 phonograms on flash cards and on record taught through speech, writing, spelling, and reading; therefore, all of these are taught in one program. The phonograms are excellent, but we recommend that you use The Handbook for The Writing Road to Reading or the Teacher's Edition to help you organize the material.

<u>Handbook for The Writing Road to Reading</u> by Bonnie Dettmer
   Grade: K-4 thoroughly; suggestions for higher levels
   Cost:: $4.95
   Order: Small Ventures
            3055 Mason Dr.
            Mesquite TX 75150
            (214) 681-1728

This 32-page handbook is a small overview of <u>The Writing Road to Reading</u> with daily lesson plans for each level. It is a very well-organized plan with an easy-to-use approach.
<u>Phonics Workbook</u> (Level A-F) by Modern Curriculum Press, Inc.
   Grade: 1,2,3,4,5,6 (Level A,B,C,D,E,F)
   Cost: about $4.50 each; keys $2.00 each
   Order: Modern Curriculum Press, Inc.
            13900 Prospect Road
            Cleveland, OH 44136
            1-800-321-3106

These workbooks could be used in addition to Spaulding, but not to replace it. The older levels include both phonics and work study.

SPELLING

<u>The Writing Road to Reading</u> by Romalda Bishop Spaulding

<u>Basic Goals in Spelling</u> by Kottmeyer and Claus
   Grade: 1,2,3,4,5,6,7,8
   Cost: $5.25 - $5.91 (workbooks not textbooks)
   Order: McGraw-Hill
            P.O. Box 409
            Heightstown, NJ 08520
            1-800-262-4729

Individuals can order only from the main company. If you call the phone number listed for information, you are calling the main company which handles thousands of different books. The operators are not familiar with "school books." The company *does* have the spellers, even if they "can't find them." Insist they keep looking; they are worth the effort.

LANGUAGE/GRAMMAR

<u>Language</u> (1-6) by A Beka Books
   Grade: 1,2,3,4,5,6
   Cost: $8.25 each; teacher's edition $12.75-$13.75 each
   Order: A Beka Books
            Box 18000
            Pensacola, FL 32523-9160
            (904) 478-8933

These are good grammar workbooks with all the rules in the back of each book. Highly recommended for older levels.

READING COMPREHENSION

Read, Study, Think by Weekly Reader
>Grade: K,1,2,3,4,5,6
>Cost: ?
>Order: Field Publications
>   4343 Equity Dr.
>   Columbus, OH 43216
>   1-800-999-7100

We have found these books to be excellent in testing for main idea, reading comprehension, drawing conclusions, relationships and analogies, and cause and effect. Each book contains about thirty selections.

Early Reading Comprehension in Varied Subject Matter by Jane Ervin
>Grade: Four separate books spanning grades 2-4
>Cost: $3.75 each; keys $.50 each
>Order: Educators Publishing Service, Inc.
>   75 Moulton Street
>   Cambridge, MA 02138-1104
>   1-800-225-5750

The four books (A,B,C,D) contain tests, sequencing, main idea, content comprehension, and vocabulary. Each book contains about thirty selections. Great!

Reading Comprehension in Varied Subject Matter by Jane Ervin
>Grade: 3,4,5,6,7,8,9,10,11,12
>Cost: $4.75 - $5.75 each; keys $1.00 each
>Order: Educators Publishing Service, Inc. (see above)

Each book contains thirty-one selections.

VOCABULARY

Wordly Wise by Kenneth Hodkinson and Joseph G. Ornato
>Grade: 4,5,6,7,8,9,10,11,12 (Books named 1,2,3,4,5,6,7,8,9)
>Cost: $3.75 - $4.00 each; keys $3.00 each
>Order: Educators Publishing Service, Inc. (see above)

Each lesson introduces about twelve words. Through several exercises the words are used in context, practiced in sentences, tested for multiple meanings, and beginning with Book 4, examined for root words, suffixes and prefixes, and much more. Great!

MATH

Making Math Meaningful by David Quine, The Cornerstone Curriculum Project
      Grade: K,1,2,3,4,5,6
      Cost: K = $30.00; 1-6 = $35.00
      Order: The Cornerstone Curriculum Project
                      2006 Flat Creek
                      Richardson, TX 75080
                      (214) 235-5149

This is the only math curriculum that we know that teaches concepts before calculation skills
and therefore lays the foundation for true understanding of math. This is not a drill book, so
you may want to add drill books and/or flash cards. Although this curriculum requires parent
involvement, it is written so clearly in a "What do I say?" and "What do I do?" format, that it is
easy to pick up and just start, even for Dad who just walks in the door.

When to Introduce What Workbooks
(merely suggested)

Grade K   Alphabet Activities
Spaulding
Math
(all of the above without writing, just enjoying)

Grade 1   Spaulding/Phonics
Spelling
Math

Grade 2   Spaulding/Phonics
Spelling
Language (if child can write sentences)
Math

Grade 3   Spaulding/Phonics (if still needed)
Spelling
Language (if writing is fluent)
Math

Grade 4   Phonics (if still needed)
Spelling
Language
Reading Comprehension
Vocabulary (don't overload)
Math

Grade 5   Spelling
Language
Reading Comprehension
Vocabulary
Math

Grade 6   Spelling
Language
Reading Comprehension
Vocabulary
Math

There are other ways that we add to KONOS. From time to time we take lessons (e.g., computer, sailing, violin), sign up for college courses (e.g., French, mechanical drawing), participate in sports, and hold jobs to supplement our KONOS program.

HOW DO I TEACH WRITING SKILLS?

Writing is a process that needs to be developed and nurtured. Keep saying to yourself, "process not product" when you begin to teach writing. If our three year old scribbles yellow marks on a page and says, "Look, Mommy, a tree," we exclaim, "How beautiful!" and slap it on the refrigerator. But woe to the child who is sent into another room with the instructions, "Write a paper." How dare that child come back and ask for help. We demand a perfectly written and punctuated paper in an hour. Why is it that we will not allow our children to <u>learn</u> the process before we demand a perfect <u>product</u>? Perhaps it is because you don't know <u>how</u> to teach the writing process. You may feel inadequate in your own writing skill. Most parents do. That is because we ourselves were insufficiently taught how to write well. We don't know the standards for great writing, we've been taught poorly, and we're out of practice. Don't worry. It isn't as difficult as it first seems. Actually there are just a few things you need to know. All you need to know is the standards of good writing, how to make writing a part of your life, and some good teaching techniques.

1) Know the standards of good writing

How can you be a good writer if you don't know what good writing is? To be a good writer you must be able to express yourself honestly, clearly, concisely, and persuasively. To do this you must know the standards of what makes good writing. We have listed the standards for what constitutes a good writer on the following pages. The best way to see these standards in practice is to read great literature. When you come across something that is beautifully, concisely, or picturesquely expressed (e.g., in a letter from a friend), read it aloud to your family. Being exposed to greatness will make it harder to settle for mediocrity.

a) Use the active voice.

The active voice is more direct than the passive voice. *I bought the book* is more forceful than *The book was bought by me*.

b) Use the positive form.

The positive form is clearer than the negative form. *He usually came late* is better than *He was not very often on time*.

c) Use definite, specific, concrete language.

Good writers create specific pictures for their readers. Rather than *fruit*, use *orange*. Rather than *foreigner*, use *Italian*. Rather than *play*, use *comedy*. Rather than *sound*, use *cry*. When writing sentences, do the same. Instead of *A period of unfavorable weather set in,* use *It rained every day for a week.* Instead of *He showed satisfaction as he took possession of his well-earned reward,* use *He grinned as he pocketed his fifty-cent piece.*

d) Be concise.

Vigorous writing omits needless words. Consider these needless words, for example: *liquid oil, wealthy millionaire, scaly fish, lethal bullet,* and *dead corpse*. Phrases can be shortened. Good writers add *ly, able, ness,* and *ful* to words, thus omitting needless words. For example, substitute the following:

For *there is no doubt but that,* use *doubtlessly*.
For *in a hasty manner,* use *hastily*.
For *this is a subject that,* use *this subject*.

For *he is a man who,* use *he.*
For *the fact that he had not succeeded,* use *his failure.*

Sentences can be shortened by using apositives (little phrases in commas behind a noun). Instead of *My dog is the one that is barking. He comes when I call,* use *My dog, the one barking, comes when I call.* Instead of *My sister is the girl wearing a blue dress. She is in the fifth grade,* use *My sister, the girl wearing the blue dress, is in the fifth grade.* Sentences can also be shortened by using prepositional phrases instead of whole clauses. A prepositional phrase is a combination of a preposition (e.g., at, in, with, between, before, on) with a noun. Instead of *When you come to the third traffic light, turn left,* use *At the third traffic light, turn left.* Instead of *While we were having dinner, he started an argument,* use *During dinner he started an argument.* Instead of *As soon as spring arrives, we'll go to the lake,* use *In the spring we'll go to the lake.*

e) Keep the same tense.

Contrast the next two paragraphs. The first is using three tenses (present, past, and future). The second uses the same tense (present).

> *My dog is a clever animal. He buried his bones in the dirt to keep the cat from finding them. The cat will have to look hard to find them.*

> *My dog is a clever animal. He buries his bones in the dirt to keep the cat from finding them. The cat looks hard to find them.*

f) Use colorful nouns and verbs.

A good writer uses $1.00 words rather than 10¢ words. One colorful noun or verb is worth far more than many descriptive words (adjectives and adverbs). Which word is worth more: *walked* or *ambled, said* or *stuttered, asked* or *interrupted, good* or *a gold mine?* Instead of *The betting man claimed that he had won,* substitute *The braggart touted his winnings.* Instead of *The rich house had beautiful furniture,* substitute *The mansion was furnished for a king.*

g) Vary language.

Instead of repeating the same word over and over, use a thesaurus to find a synonym. When writing about a quarrel, use words like *fight, disagreement, feud, squabble,* and/or *rift.*

h) Keep related words together.

The classic *Throw Mama from the train a kiss* is an example of separating words and causing confusion (and laughter). Contrast the following examples:

> *He noticed a large stain in the rug that was right in the middle.*
> *He noticed a large stain right in the middle of the rug.*

> *There was a stir in the audience that suggested disapproval.*
> *A stir of disapproval was in the audience.*

i) Place the most emphatic word at the beginning of the sentence.

If you put the most forceful word at the end of a sentence, it loses its punch. *This steel is principally used for making razors, because of its hardness* is less effective than *Because of its hardness, this steel is used in making razors.*

j) Use a mixture of description, explanation, facts, statistics, reasons, comparisons, contrasts, feelings, and impressions.

My Adventurous Flight
by Jason (a very advanced eight-year-old)

As we began to dive, I felt my stomach jump into my throat. Our pilot told us that the Grand Canyon floor was one mile below. I wondered if our Cessna 207 would hold together as we neared the canyon floor. Our pilot Steve told me to tell him when to turn and I said "Turn!"

As we flew over the Colorado River Steve told us some of the rapids were 12-25 feet high. Two years ago my uncle rafted down the Colorado River with 20 other people. He said the ride was awesome. Our family had reservations for rafting but had to cancel them.

The rock formations we flew past were named for how they looked. One rock formation was called The Scorpion. Another was Snoopy. As we were flying by I saw why they had those names. Snoopy looked like he was sunbathing on the rock.

The flight might be over in real life, but not in my memory. What had started as just a river had become the Grand Canyon.

Jason incorporated the following characteristics to make his paper a good paper:

(1) Specific (*one mile*) and detailed (*Cessna 207*) with facts (*rapids 12-25 feet*)

(2) Vivid descriptions (*dive* rather than *fly*; *stomach jumped into my throat* rather than *I was scared*)

(3) Quotes (*Turn!*)

(4) Information (*uncle rafted..., We had reservations...*)

(5) Reasoning (why rock formations have certain names, what carved the canyon)

(6) Comparing (flight is over but not the memory)

(7) Emotions (memory and *stomach in throat*)

(8) Clincher ending (*What had started...*)

k) Connect ideas.

A good composition has a variety of kinds of sentences—simple sentences (*I make my bed. I tidy up my room.*), complex sentences (using clauses like <u>When</u> *I'm finished making my bed, I'll pick up my room*), and compound sentences (*I make my bed <u>and</u> I tidy* *up my room* or *I make my bed then tidy up my room*). Practice using the following words to tie sentences together:

and	besides	also
first	next	then
finally	above	below
but	still	on the other hand
in fact	for instance	in short
furthermore	eventually	nevertheless
indeed	consequently	to be sure
to sum up		

For example, C.J. (age 11) wrote in his comparison of Handel and Mozart:

While Mozart was encouraged to compose, Handel was prohibited from composing. Handel used his music to praise the Lord, whereas Mozart didn't praise the Lord with his music.

You can also tie together two sentences by focusing on one word. For example, note the use of "soothe" and "harp" in the following two sentences:

David soothed the sheep with his harp. Later he soothed Saul's spirit with his harp.

Another way to hang ideas together is to keep related sentences together. Just by their proximity, it is understood that one follows another. In the following example, there is no need for the word "then."

He slowly walked across the hall. Then he took out his key and opened the door.

l) Use paragraphs to separate ideas.

To mark a break between two groups of ideas, start a new paragraph, but be sure to connect paragraphs with transitional sentences so that there is a smooth shifting of gears. One way to do this is to carry over a word or idea from one paragraph to the next.

Jason wrote:

One day a man came to Pasteur and said, "My wine has been turning bad lately." From this time on he devoted his life to the study of germs.

Pasteur tried many ways of killing germs....

Carson wrote:

(end of first paragraph) *...The boy, assured that all was safe, went to bed.*

(beginning of second paragraph) *While he was asleep, the fire alarm sounded...*

In his Handel-Mozart comparison, C.J. wrote about the similarities of Handel and Mozart in the first paragraph. The second paragraph started with *In some ways, however, they were very different.* He went on to discuss the differences between Handel and Mozart.

m) Place the strongest idea last.

Use a kick or wrap-up idea to climax the paper. We shouldn't have to ask if the paper is over.

Jason finished his Pasteur paper with *Pasteur died at the age of 74. He is, however, very much alive today because of his institutes.* C.J. finished his Handel-Mozart paper with *Although Mozart and Handel had some similarities, they had more differences.*

n) Stick to your subject.

Every paragraph in a good composition should point back to the title of the paper. If it is irrelevant, omit it.

Remember these are the standards of an <u>excellent</u> writer, who learned them gradually and practiced them long. They are not learned and practiced in a year. Teach them to your children gradually, one or just a few at a time.

2) Make writing a part of your life

Perhaps your skills are rusty, because you are out of practice. We live in an instant society with telephones, copy machines, and fax writers. No wonder we are out of practice. If you need a writing "tune-up," practice writing <u>along</u> <u>with</u> your children. One family has a writing day where everyone corresponds with friends. One family writes together every night in personal journals and diaries. Make writing enjoyable by listening to pleasant music. Make it easy by providing stationery, clipboards, colored pens, and pencils. Read to your children what you have written and ask them to edit <u>your</u> work. Practice, practice, practice to become a good writer.

INFORMAL WRITING	FORMAL WRITING
Emphasis on the process of writing	Emphasis on the end product
Quantity— proofread but not revised and recopied	Quality— proofread, revised, recopied
Letters, diaries, experiences recorded, inspirations, etc.	Reports, book reports, essays, etc.
Emphasis on content only	Emphasis on content plus spelling, punctuation, capitalization, and form

There are two kinds of writing—**informal** and **formal**. **Informal** writing is the writing of letters, lists, diaries, and notes. It is the kind of writing that is done primarily for yourself where little editing and almost no re-writing is required. It is not to be submitted for a grade or as a public document. **Formal** writing, on the other hand, is what we usually associate with school papers. These stories and reports need to be edited, revised, and rewritten. Young children need to practice more **informal** writing; older children need to practice more **formal** writing.

Whether **formal** or **informal** writing, write much and vary the the kinds of writing you do. Some of the kinds of papers that you will want your children to write (over time) are the following:

biographies	description of a musical composition
autobiographies	description of an experience
summary of story	agreement or disagreement of an idea
poetry	summary of an experience
book reports	directional paper ("how to" paper)
stories	persuasive paper (taking a position like "Why Home School")
editorials	factual paper (e.g., newspaper reporting)
advertisements	comparison and contrast
interviews	letters (personal, business)
dialogues	description of a picture
scripts	descripton of a person
research papers	

3) Use good teaching techniques

Most of us were taught using poor teaching techniques. A faulty assumption was that if we knew the mechanics of language we would be good writers. To be a good writer, however, requires more than just completing workbooks in language arts. Knowing the mechanics of capitalization, punctuation, spelling, and grammar is to good writing what knowing the parts of a car is to good driving. Knowing the parts is important but insufficient. To be a good writer requires actual writing, not just filling in blanks in workbooks.

Another mistake was grading our work but not coaching us in how to improve our writing. To coach your own children, use these techniques:

a) Teach content first, mechanics second.

You've heard us say that children learn best by seeing the big picture first before concentrating on the specific. This is true, too, in teaching writing. Who cares what a complex sentence is before becoming a fluent writer? Once he is able to write a paragraph, however, he will see that a mere series of simple sentences is boring. Including compound and complex sentences makes his paper more interesting. When your child can write whole paragraphs fluently, he will be ready to learn the mechanics of how to improve his written composition. So, teach the mechnics of language within the content of what your child has written. In other words, have your child write a flow of thoughts or ideas. Then revise his spelling, sentence structure, grammar, vocabulary, capitalization, and punctuation.

b) Write from first-hand experience.

Which would be of greater meaning to your child—a report on the history of boating or a story about an actual boat trip? We believe in providing our children with first-hand experiences in order to learn best. Within the KONOS CURRICULUM you find multitudes of things to do and places to go. Have your child write about these things. Not only is this more motivating for your child, it encourages him to write from all his senses (seeing, hearing, smelling, tasting, touching). The closer the experience, the more real it is to the writer. If it is not possible to actually be there (for example when studying a period of history), pretend to be there. When Carson wrote about Marco Polo's travels, he wrote a story from the camel's perspective. In this way he imagined what the camel saw, heard, smelled, tasted, and felt. Likewise, in the Weather sub-unit he wrote a story pretending to be a raindrop taking a trip through a weather cycle. When our children wrote an editorial, we assigned a topic guaranteed to motivate—"Should Children Receive Allowances?"

c) Write on subjects of interest.

If your child is interested in humor, have him write a humorous story. If he is interested in motorcycles, have him write about motorcycles. Tap into your child's "interest-bank." Why make writing more difficult than it already is? Remember one of our goals is to make learning fun, to encourage life-long learners. We want, whenever possible, to delight our children not defeat them.

d) Give specific assignments.

Experienced and confident writers can choose a topic of interest and start to write. Beginner writers, however, become confused with vague assignments. They panic at *Write a poem*, whereas *Write a non-rhyming poem about how it feels on a snowy day* is less threatening. *Write a paragraph about the Revolutionary War using these words— Stamp Act, Minutemen, Paul Revere, and Redcoats* is less of an obstacle than *Write a paper about the Revolutionary War*.

e) Dialogue with your child.

If you want your child to write a good paper, you will have to "talk it through" with him. Not only will you have to show him what constitutes good writing, you will have to help him get there. When he writes, *The man walked home*, you, the coach, must help him to improve his sentence. "Tell me about the man," you might say. "What was he wearing?" "How did he look?" "Tell me about how he was walking." "Where was his home?" "What was it like?" "Can you make this word (e.g., walked) into a dollar word (e.g., skipped)?" When older children write, they need <u>less</u> help, but they still need help. "Get me into the story by using more action right at the start." "I can actually feel what it is like when you write about the storm." "I don't fully understand what you mean here when you write, 'She was angry.' How angry? What did she say? What did she do?" "Can you think of a better way to end the story? No? How about something like this..."

f) Help your child to evaluate his own work.

The dialogue above was helping the child to discriminate and to make judgments about his own work. Older children can evaluate their own work based on a checklist that you provide. When Jason wrote a paper about owls, he was to evaluate what he had written using the following checklist:

- Correct information
- Answering to reflect the question or topic (e.g., *Owls eat meat* rather than *He eats meat.*)
- Detailed, specific answers (e.g., *The owl does not make noise when it flies, because its wing feathers are frayed on the edges* rather than *The owl doesn't make noise when it flies because it is quiet.*)
- Listing reasons to support a statement (e.g., *An owl is an excellent hunter, because it has binocular vision, larger eyes than most animals, asymmetrical ears, and silent flight.*)
- Comparing (e.g., *A heron's bill is long and straight, while an owl's beak is short and curved downward.*)
- "Dollar words" (e.g., *regurgitate* vs. *vomit*, *acute hearing* vs. *good hearing*, *talons* vs. *feet*)
- Colorful adjectives (e.g., *piercing eyes, grip-like feet, swooping wings*)
- Centered title
- Correct right and left margins
- Page numbers

61

- Neat writing
- Complete sentence answers
- Varied sentence structure (e.g., compound, simple, complex)
- Correct punctuation
- Correct capitalization
- Correct spelling
- Good opening, closing, and transition sentences

Older children can also evaluate the work of other authors. Let them edit each others' work. Eight-year-old C.J. remarked to his dad, a science writer, "Don't worry about making mistakes on your article, Dad. Mom and I will help you edit it."

4) Teach to your child's stage of writing

STAGES OF WRITING

Some elements of this chart are from GROWING UP WRITING by Linda Leonard Lamme

Listening & Speaking	Beginning Reader & Writer	Transitional Writer	Fluent Writer
Birth - Kindergarten	Grades 1 - 3	Grades 3 - 6	Grades 7 - Adult
• Auditory, Oral stage • Listens to adults' word patterns and tries to imitate them • Names objects • Begins talking • Begins recalling events and telling what happened • Sequences events • Scribbles and colors • Learns by investigating and experimenting	• Broad stage moving from letter formation to paragraph formation • Slow, belabored, dependent writing • Poor spelling • Inconsistent letter forms, capitalization & punctuation (if any) • Letter reversal or writing backwards • Little recognition of errors • Interested in expression, just writing ideas down • Interested in the process	• Faster & more independent writing • More uniform letters, capitalization, and punctuation • Easy error recognition because of awareness of the standard • Proofreads own work • Sees writing as more complex • Discouraged easily • Taxed by longer pieces • Interested in getting ideas on the paper, plus the form • Interested in the process and product	• Fluent writing • Independent writing • Consistent letter forms, capitalization and punctuation • Self evaluating and correcting (in part) • Uses the entire writing process of prewrite, compose, edit • Interested in ideas and form • Interested in the product

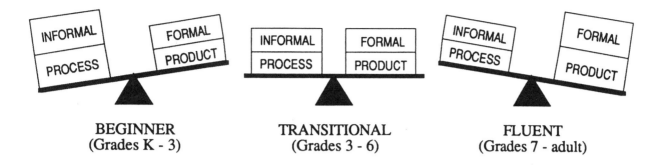

BEGINNER
(Grades K - 3)

TRANSITIONAL
(Grades 3 - 6)

FLUENT
(Grades 7 - adult)

We will give you ideas on how to teach to each stage of writing.

Listening and Speaking Stage

During this stage the child is listening to people speak and learning how to express himself. He hears new words, how words fit together to make sentences, and how ideas are organized. He experiments with speech, first trying to say words, then phrases, then sentences, then whole paragraphs. He inquisitively asks, "Wassat?" ("What's that?") as he points to articles around the house.

Having collected a repertoire of words, he then tries his hand (or tongue) at saying these words. From there he begins to put words together to complete an idea. For example, for "The dog rolled the ball under the car" he may say, "Dog ball car." For "The baby knocked the chair down" he may say, "Baby chair down." Later he experiments with phrases. Now for "The dog rolled the ball under the car" he may say, "Dog ball under car." For "The baby knocked the chair down," he may now say, "Baby knock chair down." He persistently tries to imitate the speech of adults, although he makes many errors. He may say something like, "Dog roll ball under car. Me go get ball." Finally, he can say, "The dog rolled the ball under the car. I went to get the ball."

What is a child learning during this stage? He is learning vocabulary and correct language usage. He is also learning how to organize his thoughts, how to evaluate his own expression, and how to correct his errors. These skills are extremely important in becoming a good writer. Through this practice he is learning the basics of outlining, composing, and editing.

How can you help your child to develop skills in this oral stage?

1) Dialogue.

The most important thing you can do at this stage is to speak and read to your child. As he listens to language properly used, he establishes a standard for correct language usage. He increases his vocabulary, hears word patterns, hears ideas presented in sequence, and builds understanding.

The second most important thing is to allow your child opportunity to speak. Be available to answer his questions. When he does ask, give precise information suitable for his age level. When you child asks, "What is wrong with that child?," you can answer with "That child has spina bifida. The nerves in his spine have been severed so that he cannot walk." Ask him questions like "What happened when you went to Johnny's house?" or "What is this?" or "Why do you think it is hot in the summer?" "Tell it back" (after reading a story together). Look at picture books and photo albums together and have him tell what is happening. Follow through on ideas he starts to express. For example, when the child says, "The dog rolled the ball under the car. I went to get it," extend the conversation by saying, "I think that dog likes to play soccer like you do. What do you think?" Or you could ask, "Where was this? When did this happen?" to encourage him to give more detail. Try to make your questions open-ended rather than yes or no questions to give him opportunity to organize his thoughts and to express more. Expand his vocabulary without correcting him. For example, say, "That frisky collie just loves to roll soccer balls. Yesterday he rolled it under the Chevrolet." In other words, take an idea and expand it using more precise vocabulary and correct language usage. After you read a story to your child, ask questions to help him to organize his thoughts, sequence the story, refine his expression, practice language usage, etc. All these skills will help immensely when he is ready to start composing papers. After Jessica had read The Littlest Bear to Rhett, she dialogued with him about what was read. These are some of the questions she asked him:

What was the little boy's name?
What is happening in this picture?
What is this called?
What did Johnny want more than anything else in the world?
What did he want on his barn? Look at the picture.
What was he planning to do to the bear? Tell me what happened.
Why did the bear go with him?
Who is "he" (after Rhett kept saying "he" without identifying who)?
What did Johnny feed the little bear? Do you want to look at the picture to help you remember?
What did Johnny's father say he had to do to the bear?
How did this make Johnny feel?
Where did he go first?
The bear fell into a what?
What was the last thing that happened?
Did the story end happily or sadly?

2) Do concrete activities.

The more your child does the more he has to talk about. Provide many different kinds of experiences. As you go through your daily activities, point out things to him (e.g., telephone wires, bank vault, pot roast, steam cleaner, cashier). Through this exposure he is developing his vocabulary and his sensory awareness. He is discriminating tastes, smells, sights, sounds, and feelings. By being physically involved in activities he is also developing his gross and fine motor skills which will help in his handwriting.

3) Dramatize.

When we say dramatize we do not mean formal dramatic productions. Rather, you can pretend to be whatever you are trying to teach. Children naturally dress up because they love to put themselves in others' shoes. Encourage this. Dramatize Bible stories (e.g., towel on head, bathrobe, sandals, stick for Moses parting the Red Sea). Dramatize nursery rhymes (e.g., have your child run to the corner when you read "Little Jack Horner sat in the corner"). Dramatize literature (e.g., put on a sleeper, make paper bunny ears, and be Peter Rabbit running away from Mr. MacGregor, Daddy with a straw hat and hoe). Young children can pantomime single words (e.g., hop, skip, silly, baby). Pantomime to play "Guess What I Am Doing." Dramatizing helps to fix a picture in the child's mind of the particular details within the story (e.g., the clothing, the foods, the climate, the specific action). For your child to dramatize what he has learned he must figure out the main points of the story, the story's sequence, and specific details. Dramatizing is one of the most basic ways to teach your child how to express himself long before he is ready to hold a pencil in his hand.

4) Play games.

Children love to play games. A wise teacher can make almost any activity into a game (e.g., "Beat the Clock" to sort the laundry). The following games will help to develop your child's language ability:

a) Go and Get

To build your child's discriminating ability, ask him to "go and get" certain objects (e.g., something red and pointed). As his skills increase, make it more difficult (e.g., something red, pointed, wooden, and old).

b) Hop to the Letter

To help your child discriminate letters write large letters on pieces of paper and arrange them randomly on the floor. Have your child hop to the correct letter as you say its sound. As your child grows in knowledge of letters, add phonograms and blends (e.g., sw, ai, spl, ow).

c) First, Second, Third

To help your child learn how to put ideas in sequence, draw pictures of a task and have child physically sequence the activities (e.g., mowing the lawn, making applesauce, doing laundry). Add activities as the child matures in sequencing ability.

d) Sort Box

To help your child distinguish and classify, lay out several boxes or plastic containers labeled for your child to sort objects. Label the box with adjectives such as red, smooth, shiny, rough. Although your child cannot read at this stage, you can read the labels to him and help him to identify the characteristics of such objects as sandpaper, aluminum foil, felt, apple, and stone.

e) Guess What I'm Holding

To help your child match adjectives to nouns (long before he knows what an adjective or a noun is), hide an object behind your back and give adjective clues (e.g., "It is blue, wooden, and pointed."). Have him guess the object. Take turns.

f) Alike and Different

Look at two objects and tell ways in which the objects are alike. Then list the ways in which the objects are different. This game helps to build discrimination, classification, and expression.

Beginning Reading and Writing

During this stage the child learns to read and write. He becomes acquainted with symbols and practices working with them. When the child is ready, there is a rapid progression of learning how to read sounds, then words, then phrases, then sentences, and finally whole paragraphs. Some children move quickly into the writing stage from here; others have more difficulty. Sometimes the physical holding of a pencil and the eye-hand coordination are not yet sufficiently developed. There is a wide range of ages at which a child is ready to read and write. As a home-schooling parent you have the advantage of teaching your child <u>at the time when</u> he is ready. The concentration during this stage should be process, not product. He will learn some spelling, some capitalization and punctuation (e.g., capital at the beginning of a sentence and a period at the end), some sentence structure (subject and predicate), and some form (e.g., when writing a letter, skip a line after the greeting and indent the first paragraph). The emphasis, however, is on the content not on the mechanics. Don't get hung up with his spelling errors. Don't worry about correcting and recopying unless the child wants to. Instead, encourage him to want to write, to see the standard of good writing, and to practice the flow of writing. Here are some ideas:

1) Dialogue.

Especially during this stage when your child is learning how to read and how to write, he needs to be hearing correct language to reinforce the standards of what constitutes good language. Talk to him and read to him. Even when he is able to read for himself, it is important that you also read to him. Reading in the initial stages can be very difficult. Make it easier by reading one page and having him read the next. As you read, you are providing an example for him of how the words should sound. You are also providing an example for voice inflection, emphasis, and flow. Without formally analyzing the form of what you read, he is hearing a standard of correct form which will help him in his writing.

2) Play "Jump to the Word."

When your child has learned initial phonics, you can reinforce what he learns by playing this game. Write words on cards and arrange them on the floor. Have him jump to the appropriate word. As your child develops, write phrases and sentences. He can also write words for you (or brothers and sisters) to play.

3) Play "Match It."

Match words with items by laying out several items and handing your child a stack of cards. Instruct him to place the correct card next to each object.

4) Make a word box of all the sight words they know.

5) Play "Mixed-up Sentences."

Write each word in a sentence on a separate card. Scramble the cards and have your child make a sentence by arranging the cards.

6) Play "The Sentence Game."

A favorite car game of ours is the Sentence Game, in which each person represents a different part of speech (e.g., adjective, noun, verb, adverb, prepositional phrase), the number depending on the number of people playing. Each person thinks of a word representing his part of speech (e.g., adjective could be "red," "soft," "exciting," or "silly;" noun could be "fire engine," "window," "sheriff," or "lawn mower"). Starting with the beginning of the sentence, each person says his word in sequence. There are some hilarious sentences that are born this way:

> *"The climbing monkey twisted excitedly down the toilet."*
> *"The embarrassed banana jump-roped slowly on the roof."*

The children are learning the parts of speech and sentence structure, all while riding to Grandma's house.

7) Play "More Specific."

Start with a word like "plant." Challenge your child to be more specific ("flower"). Keep going back and forth until you can think of nothing more specific ("plant," "flower," "rose," "American Beauty").

8) Write informally.

This is the stage for much informal writing. Label boxes, label shelves with an embosser, write grocery lists, make signs ("PRIVATE - DO NOT ENTER"), send postcards, write notes on a chalkboard, send secret messages, make greeting cards (What grandmother doesn't delight in "I LOVE YOU, GRANDMA."). Show your child how to hold a pencil and gradually introduce the formation of manuscript letters, but concentrate on the pleasure of being able to express ideas in writing. In the beginning do not correct spelling. Be less concerned with the correctness of what he writes than the content of what he writes.

9) Write answers to questions.

When he can write phrases and sentences, he is ready to answer comprehension questions. Have him write down the answers to questions about experiences and stories he has read (e.g., Charlotte's Web):

Who are the main characters in the story?
What kind of animal is Charlotte?
What kind of animal is Wilbur?
How are they different?

10) Write descriptions.

Describe a person (e.g., "Fill in the blank: 'Mommy is _____.'"). Describe a picture (e.g., a painting). Describe an experience. Describe a place (e.g., the kitchen on Saturday morning).

11) Do a commentary.

While some of the children are dramatizing or participating in a sport, have one child be an "on-the-spot reporter." While he dictates what is happening, have an older child write down what is said.

12) Write a short paper.

Once your child can write whole sentences on his own, he is ready to write a short paper, but he will need much assistance. Give him a very specific assignment based on a first-hand experience (e.g., "Yesterday at the Swimming Pool"). Talk it through with him:

"Tell me what you remember and I'll take notes for you."

"Close your eyes and tell me what you hear at the pool. What do you smell? How does it feel? What is happening?"

"Let's write a good opening sentence that will get the reader interested."

"How can you end your story? Make it a summary."

Write each idea on a separate sheet of paper or card. Then arrange the cards in sequence. As your child becomes more comfortable writing, start correcting the mechanics (i.e., spelling, grammar, vocabulary, sentence structure). At this point teach him to correct his own errors. Give him a checklist of things to check (e.g., capital at the beginning of each sentence, period at the end of each sentence). Underline in red the words mispelled and in green the words you would like replaced with better vocabulary ($1.00 words). When he gains confidence, ask him to find as many errors in his writing as he can find. Tell him you see 12 errors. Challenge him to find them.

13) Take dictation.

If your child has difficulty holding a pencil and physically writing words or is getting fatigued with writing, have him dictate to you. Have him dictate letters and stories or write a whole book for a gift. Carson wrote (at the age of 6) a book entitled <u>J.J.'s Adventures</u> for his brother's Christmas gift. He composed the whole story and drew all the illustrations, but he did not write one word. Each day we talked through a part of the book:

"Yesterday we wrote about J.J.'s building a log cabin. He is now in the woods, hungry and afraid. What happens next?

Describe what you mean by 'walked through the woods.' Good, 'crept through the woods' is more descriptive.

Tell what he is feeling. What tastes, sounds, smells, and sights are there?

You say there are wild animals attacking. Be more specific. What kind of animals? What are they like?

You say J.J. is frightened. Instead of using the word 'frightened,' tell me how he acts. You can't think of anything? Then pretend you are J.J. Act frightened. What is happening? Yes, you are shaking, your eyes are wide open, you are sweating. Let's write that down."

The whole time he is watching me print what he is dictating. He sees how the letters are formed, how words are spelled, the common denominators of every sentence (capitalized first word, a period at the end, subject (noun) and predicate (verb)), how commas are used, etc. Rather than having the mechanical skill of holding a pencil and writing get in his way, this encourages his flow of expression.

Transitional writer

The transitional writer has learned the basics of writing but is not yet fluent in being able to express his ideas in written form. He sees his errors and he sees how complex the mechanics of language is. He feels stuck and gets discouraged easily. At this point many parents make a grave mistake. They assume that because the child is able to write and knows the basic mechanics of writing, that he should be able to write independently and to produce a neat, well-constructed, finished product. In actuality, your child needs <u>more</u> help at this stage than during any other. How can you help?

1) Show him his progress.

Show him the chart of the stages of writing. Indicate to him that he has only one more stage to become fluent in writing. Let him know that it is normal to feel stuck at this stage. On the list of standards put a check next to each characteristic that he can do already. Show him work that he did in previous months. He needs to see how far he has already come.

2) Do workbooks to raise his mechanical ability.

This is the time to refine and polish mechanical abilities.

3) Coach him.

Make the process of writing as easy as possible. Be sure that his assignments are specific, that he is still writing from experience, that he is writing in areas of interest, that the standards are specific. Demonstrate to him how to write a paper. There are only three basic steps—a) pre-writing, b) composing, and c) editing, but he will need help at each step. Your job will be to provide the tissues when he child starts crying and to be the lubricator that will help get him unstuck.

Pre-writing
You must be intrinsically involved in rehearsing. First, help your child think about what he wants to write. Let ideas incubate. Brainstorm together. Then allow time to pass. Second, help him to organize his paper. One way is to draw a sun. Write the main idea in the sun. Put paragraph ideas from "rays of the sun." Or he can make a list of what he wants to include. Put ideas on different sheets of paper or note cards. Then he can sequence the ideas. Decide what he will include in each paragraph. Suppose he is writing about a trip to the zoo. The first paragraph could be on the way to the zoo, the second could be at the zoo, and the third paragraph could be on the way home from the zoo. Suppose he is writing a paper comparing owls and pigeons. Should he write one paragraph on owls and one on pigeons? Should he compare owls and pigeons characteristic by characteristic (e.g., beaks, feet, food)? Should he write one paragraph on the similarities and one paragraph on the differences? Third, help him get started with the first paragraph. Use the five W's (who, what, where, when, and why). You might tell him to write an opening sentence with a name and an action word or to write an opening sentence with an apositive and a date. Once the first sentence is written, it is easier to proceed from there.

Composing
A good writer doesn't just sit down and write. Concentration is difficult no matter what your age or experience. At this stage, it is extremely difficult. Try to keep down interruptions. Give your child large blocks of time in which to write. Provide a trash can, a glass of water, lots of paper, and sharpened pencils. Allow him to get up and stretch when needed. Even then he will get stuck. Be available for him at this point. If he is getting distracted, you need to help him get refocused. Set a mini-deadline. If he is concentrating but getting nowhere, he may need a break. But help get your child back on track. Make him succeed at the task so that he doesn't feel defeated. Be sure he knows to write a rough draft in his messiest handwriting; perfecting comes later. Don't get angry if he isn't producing. Instead try some of these ideas:

a) Have him read his paper aloud.

He will see the progress he has already made and may get himself back on track.

b) Help him to realize what is getting him stuck (e.g., sequencing, coming up with ideas, mechanics).

If mechanics are getting him stuck, put the paper up and help him with the skill. Get out the workbooks to reinforce the skill. Do it orally. For example, if he is having trouble with sequencing, do it orally all day. He must say "first," "second," "third," etc. when telling about anything.

c) Take dictation.

Just as with the beginning writer, you can help the flow of ideas by eliminating the mechanical strain. Write a paragraph that he has dictated and then let him go on with the next paragraph by himself. He can learn to do this on his own by using a tape recorder.

d) Type.

Instead of getting stuck in the handwriting process, type papers. Just the diversion of being able to use a typewriter or word processor will help some children "flow" again.

e) Use your child's learning style.

Through which sense does your child learn best? When Charles was a young student, he was taught to take notes in order to make the lesson visible. He tried for years until he finally realized he was an auditory learner. After discarding his notes, he could finally learn. The Hulcys had a tea party at their house. After the tea party, one little girl remembered the colors of the hats and the shapes of the cookies (visual), one girl talked for hours about the sweetness of the cookies and the cool drinks (tactile), one boy repeated the dialogue between the butler and the guests (auditory), while another boy told all they did like "first we sat down, then we put our napkins on our laps, then the waiter served us..." (kinesthetic or participatory). What does your child remember after an event?

Knowing your child's learning style can help you to get him "unstuck." If he is visual, write down some key words or pictures to organize his thoughts. If he is tactile, write ideas on cards and have him physically arrange them. Or he could benefit from typing his ideas. If he is auditory, let him talk through his ideas with you. "Say it aloud" is what you could instruct. If he is kinesthetic, have him act out what he is trying to write and then put words to what he is doing.

Editing
Encourage your child to find his own errors. Keep going back to the standards. At the top of the paper he is writing, put little boxes next to the standards you want him to check. Help him to replace vocabulary, correct spelling, correct punctuation and capitalization errors, rephrase and reorganize where necessary. Rewrite in his best handwriting and be sure to put it in a place of prominence for all the world to read.

Fluent Writing

The fluent writer has finally gotten over the hump of panicking when he needs to write a paper. He uses all three steps (pre-writing, composing, and editing) with some ease. His work during these stages is refinement. He needs to master the form of writing as well as punctuation and grammar. He needs help in making his writing interesting (e.g., good use of phrases, examples, similes and metaphors, climactic ending) and smooth (e.g., transitional sentences from paragraph to paragraph). At this stage he is ready to write, edit, revise, rewrite, edit, revise to produce an excellent finished product. The following are some ways you can help him most during this stage:

1) Give feedback.

Although he is now an independent writer, let him bounce his ideas off you.

2) Give him reasons to write.

Provide pen pals, publish a newspaper, or encourage him to keep a journal.

3) Refer back to the standards.

Although he has an ability to organize and express his thoughts with some mastery of the rules of language, there is still a lot of work to becoming an excellent writer. Note on his papers when he has met a particular standard. Show him where he still needs refinement. Concentrate on choosing the best word or phrase. Jessica is working with eleven-year-old Jason, trying to refine his language as he describes a birthday party:

Mom:	Make an interesting beginning where you jump into the action.
Son:	We came to the table to eat.
Mom:	Let's get specific. How many boys?
Son:	Six
Mom:	Six boys came to the table to eat. Use a better word than "came."
Son:	Raced
Mom:	Six boys raced to the table. Describe the food.
Son:	Hot dogs and chips
Mom:	Six boys raced to the table for hot dogs and chips.

To further help you instruct your child in writing, refer to the following books:

Growing Up Writing by Linda Leonard Lamne (the process)
Elements of Style by William Strunk, Jr. and E.G. White (the standards)
Any Child Can Write by Harvey Weiner (great ideas)
Learning Grammar Through Writing by Sandra M. Bell and James I. Wheeler, Educators Publishing Service, Inc., 75 Moulton Street, Cambridge, MA 02238 (manual of grammar, punctuation, capitalization)
BUILDING A GOOD WRITER THE KONOS WAY (a two-cassette tape series by KONOS)

Be patient. Know that one must walk before he can run. Start wherever your child is. Will this happen in one year? No. As your child learns step-by-step, he will gradually progress up the mountain until he reaches the pinnacle of excellence.

WHAT SKILLS SHOULD MY CHILD ACCOMPLISH EACH YEAR?

Every school district has a scope and sequence of what is covered at each grade level. As discussed above, it does not matter at what level a child learns the parts of the ear, bird behavior, or the states, as long as he does, in fact, have some knowledge of each of these sometime during his elementary school years. For math and language, however, it does matter what is taught at each level, because each level lays a foundation for the next. In learning math skills, for example, there is a sequence ("line upon line, precept upon precept") for adequately building the child's ability to reason and to calculate. To be thorough and to provide an adequate base for the next level, it is important to know what skills your child should possess at each level. Please note that we say "level," not "grade" or "age," knowing that some children start earlier than others and some progress faster than others. This is especially true from kindergarten through third grade. What is important is the sequence, not the absolute age. Use the following checklist to plan for your year and to check off skills as they are learned.

MATH AND LANGUAGE CHECKLIST
FOR GRADES K-8

KINDERGARTEN

MATH

- ❑ Count through 20
- ❑ Arrange numbers 1-10 in sequence
- ❑ Match same numbers of objects
- ❑ Add concrete objects
- ❑ Subtract (take away) concrete objects
- ❑ Classify objects by color
- ❑ Classify objects by size
- ❑ Classify objects by shape
- ❑ Contrast objects by function (i.e., use)
- ❑ Compare and classify objects by the following:

    Higher or lower
    Bigger or smaller
    Fatter or thinner
    Darker or lighter

LANGUAGE

- ❑ Focus attention on a speaker without interrupting
- ❑ Follow a simple story line as you read to him
- ❑ Respond to a story by drawing or painting what he hears
- ❑ Dramatize a story he has heard
- ❑ Tell back a story he has heard
- ❑ Tell what a story is about
- ❑ Arrange events of a story in sequential order
- ❑ Distinguish between fiction (make-believe) and non-fiction (real)
- ❑ Relate an experience he has had in complete sentences
- ❑ Supply a missing word as you tell a story
- ❑ Discriminate phonetic sounds (e.g., b, d, t, p)
- ❑ Discriminate between shapes, forms, and letters
- ❑ Follow oral directions with three or four steps (e.g., "Brush your teeth," "say good-night to Daddy," "shut off the light," and "crawl into bed")
- ❑ Memorize Bible verses, nursery rhymes, and simple songs
- ❑ Know and dramatize the following prepositions:

over	under
between	on
in front of	behind
inside	outside
next to	top
bottom	

❏ Sort a picture story into "first," "middle," and "last"
❏ Identify what is happening in a picture
❏ Recognize and imitate many different sounds, e.g. that of a:

bird	cow
dog	piano
horn	bell

❏ Recall basic information:

his full name
his parents' names
his address
his telephone number
his age
his birthday
days of the week
months of the year

❏ Name the missing parts of a picture
❏ Match pictures, letters, shapes
❏ Complete simple puzzles
❏ Play simple matching games like "Go Fish" or "Memory"
❏ Read his name

GRADE 1

MATH

❑ Read and write numbers to 100
❑ Count by 1's, 2's, 5's, and 10's to 100
❑ Know ordinal numbers (first through tenth)
❑ Know the following terms and be able to use them (e.g., "I'm thinking of a number; it is greater than 12 but lesser than 18. What could it be?")

        Greater than
        Lesser than
        Equal to

❑ Group objects into sets (e.g., two sets containing 10 Legoes and 5 Legoes is the same as three sets containing 5 Legoes each)
❑ Add numbers up to 20 (without regrouping or carrying)
❑ Subtract numbers up to 20 (without regrouping or borrowing)
❑ Solve simple math problems using manipulatives
❑ Measure to the nearest inch or centimeter
❑ Measure feet, yards
❑ Tell time to the nearest half-hour
❑ Recognize dates on a calendar
❑ Tell temperature
❑ Recognize halves and fourths using concrete objects (e.g., measuring cup, 1/2 cookie)
❑ Know the value of penny, nickel, dime and play store with money giving the correct amounts for purchases

LANGUAGE

❑ Follow a story line involving several characters
❑ Understand the feelings and emotions of characters
❑ Identify the main idea in a story
❑ Speak clearly and at an appropriate rate
❑ Contribute ideas in a group discussion
❑ Sequence events correctly when telling a true story
❑ Dictate a fictional story
❑ Dictate a true story
❑ Use correct forms of regular nouns and verbs when speaking
❑ Select topics that would interest other people
❑ Present a poem within a group
❑ Give a short sequence of directions for others to follow
❑ Read short, common words correctly (if they follow phonetic rules)
❑ Figure out a word by using context clues
❑ Alphabetize using the initial letter
❑ Identify the cause of an event
❑ Learn basic phonetic spelling
❑ Identify a sentence

❏ Dictate a simple story
❏ Capitalize the first word in a sentence
❏ Put a period at the end of a sentence
❏ Put a question mark at the end of a question
❏ Write legible manuscript letters
❏ Write lists (e.g., names, grocery items)
❏ Add "s" to make plurals

GRADE 2

MATH

- ❑ Read and write numbers to 1000
- ❑ Distinguish between odd and even numbers
- ❑ Know that odd numbers cannot be divided in half
- ❑ Add numbers horizontally and vertically and in a variety of sequences (e.g., 2+3+5 and 5+2+3) and know they are of the same value
- ❑ Know money values (penny, nickel, dime, quarter, half-dollar, dollar)
- ❑ Recognize equal values of money (e.g., 10 pennies equals one dime; 10 dimes equals one dollar) to reinforce place value
- ❑ Add with regrouping (carrying)
- ❑ Read 1/2, 1/3, 1/4
- ❑ Tell time to the nearest quarter hour
- ❑ Locate a date on the calendar
- ❑ Use simple graphs and charts to solve problems
- ❑ Measure with inches and centimeters
- ❑ Measure with quarts, cups, pints, and liters

LANGUAGE

- ❑ Adjust his environment to keep from getting distracted (e.g., turn off the radio)
- ❑ Identify the main idea in a speaker's message
- ❑ Describe the time and setting of a story
- ❑ Speak clearly to a group
- ❑ Stay on the topic when speaking
- ❑ Narrate events in chronological order
- ❑ Read aloud to a group using appropriate cadence and stress
- ❑ Read silently
- ❑ Ask thoughtful questions of a person who has spoken about a topic
- ❑ Relate events orally using description of characters, places, and events
- ❑ Recall facts from a story or event shared previously
- ❑ Tell the cause and the effect within a story
- ❑ Read using initial blends, digraphs, and diphthongs
- ❑ Figure out a meaning from context clues (e.g., "It's cold; close the ____.")
- ❑ Alphabetize using the first two letters of a word
- ❑ Follow written directions
- ❑ Write a simple letter
- ❑ Write simple poetry
- ❑ Write one and two-sentence answers to comprehension questions
- ❑ Locate errors in his own writing (e.g., failure to capitalize the first word in a sentence, failure to put a period at the end of a sentence, words left out, wrong spelling)
- ❑ Rewrite rough drafts
- ❑ Write complete sentences without coaching
- ❑ Punctuate sentences with period, question mark, or exclamation point at the end
- ❑ Write legible manuscript letters
- ❑ Use correct forms of adjectives and adverbs

GRADE 3

MATH

- ❏ Read and write numbers to the ten-thousands
- ❏ Know place values (1, 10, 100, 1000)
- ❏ Add numbers in the hundreds with regrouping (carrying)
- ❏ Subtract numbers in the hundreds with regrouping (borrowing)
- ❏ Know that multiplication is a simple form of addition (e.g., 2+2+2 = 3x2 = 6)
- ❏ Determine whether to add, subtract, multiply, or divide in word problems
- ❏ Do simple multiplication problems (e.g., "If there are four people and each has two puppies, how many puppies do they have all together?")
- ❏ Round numbers to nearest 10 and 100
- ❏ Estimate the answer to addition and subtraction problems by rounding to the nearest 10 and 100; check answers
- ❏ Know ordinal numbers first through hundredth
- ❏ Tell time to the nearest minute
- ❏ Add and subtract time
- ❏ Measure inches, feet, yards, centimeters, meters, cups, pints, quarts, gallons, milliliters, and liters
- ❏ Add and subtract money (cents to dollars)
- ❏ Solve problems using bar graphs and charts
- ❏ Figure out what information is missing to solve a problem
- ❏ Find the perimeter of a square, rectangle, triangle or other shape
- ❏ Use a calculator

LANGUAGE

- ❏ Adjust physical conditions to promote listening (e.g., moving chair closer to speaker)
- ❏ Recognize the purpose of a presentation (e.g., to give advice, to entertain, to sell)
- ❏ Respond to a speaker by asking questions and providing pertinent information
- ❏ Distinguish between fact and opinion
- ❏ Create dramatic portrayals of people
- ❏ Use visual aids in making oral presentations
- ❏ Give reasons when trying to persuade
- ❏ Read stories and poems expressively
- ❏ Know basic sight vocabulary
- ❏ Add "d" and "ed" endings
- ❏ Use "may" and "can" correctly
- ❏ Recognize synonyms (e.g., lady/woman, boy/lad, plate/dish, wish/hope, have faith/believe) and homonyms (e.g., knead/need, read/red, read/reed, sew/so)
- ❏ Know what a noun is and give examples
- ❏ Know what a verb (action word) is and give examples
- ❏ Know what an adjective (describing word) is and give examples
- ❏ Use a dictionary to find meanings and pronunciations
- ❏ Understand the meaning of words in context
- ❏ Recall important facts in a story that support the main idea
- ❏ Summarize a story
- ❏ Understand the multiple causes of an event

❑ Predict probable future outcomes in a story (i.e., "What do you think happened next?")
❑ Draw conclusions
❑ Follow two and three-step directions
❑ Read orally with fluency, expression and nonverbal communication
❑ Use parts of a book: index, glossary
❑ Use an encyclopedia to find information
❑ Use a telephone book
❑ Use graphic sources (e.g., maps, graphs, diagrams, globes, pictures) for information
❑ Differentiate between figurative (i.e., simile and metaphor) and literal language
❑ Follow a plot in a story that is not chronological
❑ Expand topics by collecting information from a variety of resources
❑ Classify differences and likenesses of objects and events
❑ Break words into syllables to better read and spell
❑ Write legible cursive letters
❑ Join related sentences into paragraphs
❑ Indent the first word of a paragraph
❑ Write a simple book review
❑ Write a story telling who, what, when, where, why, and how
❑ Use correct subject-verb agreement
❑ Use period, comma, question mark, apostrophe

GRADE 4

MATH

- ❏ Read, count, and write numbers from 0 to 1,000,000
- ❏ Add any whole numbers
- ❏ Subtract any whole numbers
- ❏ Memorize multipication and division tables
- ❏ Multiply several digits
- ❏ Divide with one digit divisor, with and without remainders
- ❏ Estimate answers to multiplication and division problems
- ❏ Know Roman numerals from I to C
- ❏ Recognize spheres, cylinders, cubes, parallel lines, radius, diameter
- ❏ Know money value of all denominations
- ❏ Compare fractions with the same denominator (e.g., 1/10 is less than 3/10)
- ❏ Understand that a decimal means tenths or hundredths (e.g., 20/100 of a dollar is the same as $.20)

LANGUAGE

- ❏ Actively listen in a variety of situations
- ❏ Select from an oral presentation information needed
- ❏ Use a wide variety of words to express feelings and ideas
- ❏ Adapt the content and presentation of a speech to fit the audience
- ❏ Explain how to do something
- ❏ Present stories, plays, puns, riddles, and jokes for entertainment
- ❏ Understand word meanings by knowing a root word and adding a variety of prefixes and suffixes
- ❏ Follow multistep directions
- ❏ Read orally with ease
- ❏ Write fluently
- ❏ Write several well-constructed (i.e., correct margins, indented words, all one topic) paragraphs
- ❏ Choose a title for his story
- ❏ Correctly use quotation marks
- ❏ Edit and revise his own work
- ❏ Use the library card catalogue and encyclopedia to locate information
- ❏ Write personal letters with correct form
- ❏ Delete superfluous information from his own writing
- ❏ Use nominative, objective, and possessive forms correctly
- ❏ Correctly spell words most commonly used (See Ayres List in Spaulding's Writing Road to Reading)
- ❏ Know what an adjective is and give examples
- ❏ Use adjectives in writing sample

GRADE 5

MATH

- ❑ Estimate results
- ❑ Compute averages
- ❑ Divide and multiply using multiple digits
- ❑ Do long division
- ❑ Add fractions
- ❑ Subtract fractions
- ❑ Know the following geometric concepts:

arc	centers
circumference	semicircle
polygon	cone
pyramid	prism
congruent figure	incongruent figure

- ❑ Measure temperature using Fahrenheit and Celsius scales
- ❑ Convert measurements (pints, quarts gallons, milliliters, liters)
- ❑ Add and subtract money using decimals
- ❑ Make change
- ❑ Multiply money
- ❑ Know time measurements from seconds to years
- ❑ Measure and calculate elapsed time
- ❑ Read and use percentages

LANGUAGE

- ❑ Follow the logical organization of an oral presentation
- ❑ Detect the use of propaganda or exploitation
- ❑ Distinguish between formal and informal (colloquial) language and their proper uses
- ❑ Explain the feelings of characters
- ❑ Make wise judgments about what is heard and read
- ❑ Make organized oral presentations
- ❑ Use a set of reasons to persuade a group
- ❑ Participate on committees for problem-solving in groups
- ❑ Compose a play
- ❑ Use parts of a book: preface, copyright page
- ❑ Use a wide variety of graphic sources (e.g., maps and globes, charts and graphs, timelines, pictures and diagrams, scale drawings, transportation schedules) for information
- ❑ Adjust method and rate of reading according to purpose
- ❑ Write first and third-person stories
- ❑ Write personal letters and envelopes with correct form
- ❑ Prioritize facts in order of importance
- ❑ Spell increasingly complex words
- ❑ Use correct subject-verb agreement
- ❑ Use correct forms of regular and common irregular verbs

❑ Use adverbs in writing sentences
❑ Use similes and metaphors
❑ Know restrictions against using double negatives (e.g., "He don't hardly...," "I don't have none.")

GRADE 6

MATH

- ❑ Read, count, order, and write numbers to the billions
- ❑ Round any number to its nearest place
- ❑ Factor prime numbers
- ❑ Use decimals to the thousandth's place
- ❑ Add decimals
- ❑ Subtract decimals
- ❑ Find percentages
- ❑ Multiply fractions
- ❑ Divide fractions
- ❑ Know metric measurements
- ❑ Measure angles and arcs
- ❑ Identify types of triangles
- ❑ Calculate areas of triangles and rectangles

LANGUAGE

- ❑ Determine a speaker's motive, bias, point of view
- ❑ Use a wide and appropriate variety of rate, volume, and physical movement in oral presentation
- ❑ Respond to others in conversation by clarifying their throughts
- ❑ Use a dictionary to determine word origins and histories
- ❑ Use and write footnotes and appendices
- ❑ Write a simple bibliography
- ❑ Use periodicals and reference works to locate information
- ❑ Use an atlas; locate places by longitude and latitude
- ❑ Recognize and use personification in stories
- ❑ Include a wide variety of sentences in paragraphs
- ❑ Write business letters using correct form
- ❑ Use quotations with certain titles
- ❑ Use semicolons and colons properly
- ❑ Use all parts of speech effectively
- ❑ Use "well" and "good" appropriately
- ❑ Identify direct objects of verbs

GRADE 7

MATH

❏ Multiply using decimals
❏ Divide using decimals
❏ Understand and use exponents of positive numbers
❏ Determine the greatest common factor and the least common multiple
❏ Understand and use proportions
❏ Calculate square roots
❏ Know names of angles (right, obtuse, etc.)
❏ Find perimeters and areas of rectangles, triangles, parallelograms, and circles
❏ Bisect angles

LANGUAGE

❏ Plan and write a research paper
❏ Take notes from written text and oral presentation
❏ Outline
❏ Write for a variety of purposes and audiences
❏ Use punctuation and capitalization appropriately (e.g., commas around apositives, commas to set off name of person, commas to separate quotations of direct address, commas to set off dependent clauses, commas to set off independent clauses with direct subjects, parentheses)
❏ Use formal and informal language appropriately
❏ Substitute specific words for general words
❏ Produce well-formed sentences with variety
❏ Omit sentence fragments, run-on sentences, nonagreement between subject and verb, and faulty tense changes
❏ Proofread for punctuation, spelling, and syntax
❏ Recognize folk literature, legends, and myths
❏ Recognize an author's purpose, point of view, and opinion
❏ Know formal parts of speech; diagram sentences (See <u>Learning Grammar Through Writing</u> by Sandra M. Bell and James I. Wheeler)

> Subject/predicate
> Simple and perfect verb tenses
> Transitive and intransitive verbs
> Regular and irregular verbs
> Classifications of adjectives (descriptive, possessive, proper)
> Articles as adjectives
> Predicate adjectives
> Possessive pronouns as modifiers
> Adjective and adverbial clauses
> Prepositional phrases
> Conjunctions
> Interjections

❏ Take responsibility for managing his time to complete a written project

GRADE 8

MATH

- ❏ Use and convert fractions, decimals, percentages
- ❏ Order numbers with exponents
- ❏ Write mathematical sentences with multiple operations
- ❏ Work with negative numbers
- ❏ Know the rules of associative and distributive property (algebra)
- ❏ Draw to scale
- ❏ Calculate volumes of solid shapes (cubes, cylinders, cones, pyramids)
- ❏ Use Pythagorean theorem for finding lengths of sides of triangles
- ❏ Find surface area of solids
- ❏ Do simple statistics (range, mean, median, mode)

LANGUAGE

- ❏ Write a short novel
- ❏ Describe plot, setting, characters, and moods
- ❏ Avoid cliches and trite expressions
- ❏ Proofread for clarity of language, appropriate word choice, and effective sentences
- ❏ Use appropriate technical vocabulary for specific topic
- ❏ Choose the appropriate meaning of multimeaning words
- ❏ Participate in group discussions
- ❏ Know Greek and Latin prefixes and roots
- ❏ Use all parts of a book: visual aids, chapter headings and subheadings, italics, color coding, marginal notes, footnotes, jacket summaries, appendices
- ❏ Identify and correctly use verb tenses (e.g., present, past, past perfect, future perfect)
- ❏ Identify and correctly use infinitive, participle, gerund, predicate nominative, predicate adjective, direct and indirect object (See Learning Grammar Through Writing by Sandra M. Bell and James I. Wheeler

HOW DO I CO-OP WITH OTHER FAMILIES?

Is it necessary to co-op in order to use KONOS? No, KONOS was designed for use within family units. Many families have found, however, that there are added benefits of co-oping, such as:

1) Shared time and energy

Aren't there days when you wish someone would help you teach your children? You want to offer them all the best, but you don't have the energy or the time to give them all you want. When co-oping with other families, one mother can take all the children to her house, plan all the activities, gather all the supplies, enthusiastically teach the children, and clean up afterwards. Meanwhile, you can do those things that easily get overlooked like getting your hair cut, going to the dentist, reading a book, or lying down!

2) Shared talents

When we first started home-schooling, the Hulcys, Thaxtons, and Quines met every week. On Tuesday afternoon Wade did a P.E. class with the kids, on Wednesdays Carole took the kids for a field trip or special event, and on Thursday afternoons Shirley taught art. Later, we co-oped with several families just once weekly and had a KONOS Day. The parents chose the activities that they preferred leading. Each of us seemed to have an area of strength (art, science, drama, music, writing, countries/cultures). How wonderful for the children to have access to strengths that individually we did not have.

3) Feedback

After the initial time of developing trust and genuine caring for each other, this information can be so valuable. Parents, especially those who spend all their time with their children, tend to have tunnel vision about their own children. It is easy to miss certain weaknesses and strengths that our children have. These show up within a group in contrast to the other children. Other mothers can notice what we may not see. "Your child has a wonderful ability to problem-solve." "He tends to interrupt others when they are talking." "Maybe your son should take music lessons; he has an ear for music." "Within the group he is usually on the sidelines. How can we encourage him to gt more involved with the others?" You, as teacher, will also receive feedback and encouragement about your teaching skills.

4) Emotional and prayer support

These are the people with whom you have a bonding. They understand. Whereas others may try to understand, these are friends that have been in the trenches and can give genuine compassion. Because of your love for each other, you will want to pray for each other and for each other's children.

5) Modeling

All of us want our children exposed to godly people. What a blessing to have other families that model Christlikeness to our children.

6) Reinforced learning

When several people are assigned to report on an Indian tribe and each family takes a different one, there is the benefit to all who participate. When Patrick comes dressed in his cedar clothes with a carved totem pole and reports on the Northwest Indians, all the children learn something about the Northwest Indians. When Troy makes a headdress and reports on the Sioux Indians, all learn about the Plains Indians.

7) Instant audience

Occasionally you will want your children to do a dramatic presentation or practice public speaking or sing in chorus. By having a group like this, they not only can practice together but have a ready-made audience.

8) Hand-picked kids

One of the advantages of home-schooling is to choose godly influences for our children. This includes our children's peers. Instead of isolating them from peers through whom they can learn valuable social skills, we choose the peers with whom we want them to associate. The right kind and amount of peer pressure can be great.

If you do choose to co-op, here are some guidelines on how to co-op using KONOS.

1) Choose the people with whom you want to co-op.

Since co-oping with other families is like a marriage, you want to choose parents and children with whom you share goals, methods, views on discipline, and level of commitment. Be sure you like them and your children like their children. Be sure to observe the interaction between all the children before making a commitment to co-op together.

2) Schedule a parents' meeting during the summer.

Decide the following:

a) What kind of co-op do you want? There are several options:

(1) Field trips

Some families meet only for field trips. If the KONOS group is all using the same volume, a yearly schedule of field trips can be set up during the summer.

(2) Weekly co-op

During one full day (9:00 - 3:30) each week from 4-8 kids meet at the home of a KONOS mom for co-oping activities. This kind of co-op could have an older, middle, and/or younger group meeting simultaneously, each studying the same topic but at their own levels. All the children meet at the home of the mom teaching the older children. The other two teaching moms pick up their respective co-op groups there and take them to their homes to teach for the day. This lessens the number of carpools necessary to get the kids to the right homes.

(3) Bi-weekly co-op

Every other week the kids meet for a full day of KONOS activities.

(4) Planning

Some groups meet to plan their year together. They may plan field trips and special events to be shared.

b) Do you want to split the co-op into younger and older groups?

We've found that the best way to divide the co-op into levels is to group the readers and non-readers or the concrete thinkers and the abstract thinkers. K-3 and 4-7 are usually good group levels.

c) How shall we discipline the kids?

We use a point system that gives points for positive behaviors (e.g., finishing work, concentrating, encouraging another student) and subtracts points for negative behaviors (e.g., interrupting, speaking rudely, fighting). The children bring home their point totals; the parents use the points as they wish. Of course there is free communication between the parents. As long as you have the same standards for behavior, the parents should appreciate feedback about how their child is doing.

d) How much money should we spend?

Set limits on how much you want to spend for each unit. In our co-op the mother can spend up to $10 for her unit. If there are additional costs (e.g., for field trip), the parents contribute what is needed.

e) How much father involvement do you want?

Decide if you want fathers and children to do special activities (e.g., a military bivouac) together. How often do you want all-family activities (e.g., a Medieval Feast)?

f) Should there be assignments between co-op days?

g) Which units will be studied?

Have everyone bring a calendar. Pencil in the units you will study and when. Who will teach each topic? We have found it most successful to have two moms teach a whole topic (e.g., Indians) no matter how many weeks it lasts. It helps to have an experienced mom with a less experienced mom. These two mothers plan the sub-unit, gather the supplies, teach the activities, drive to field trips, and clean up. After designating who will teach when, these mothers meet to make general plans. By the second parents' meeting they should have a typed plan of the activities they will be doing, including dates of field trips and special events.

3) Schedule a second parents' meeting.

At this second meeting, write down all field trips and events on your calendars. Refine each sub-unit plan. Write down policies.

HOW DO I DEAL WITH MY TODDLERS?

Some home-schoolers act as if their toddlers were problems to be endured rather than a vital part of the home school. Although your life will be far more difficult if you have a toddler, it will also be richer for your other children. There are ways, however, of keeping a toddler under control to focus energy on the other children while giving your toddler what he needs.

1) Involve your toddlers.

Through the "trickle-down effect," they will amaze you with how much they learn. How much could they possibly learn if your older children were reading textbooks in another room? By doing experiential activities together, toddlers too can join in on the fun.

2) Work with your toddler first.

Either do an activity with your toddler or assign him a task before starting with the older children. Help to get him started. To decide what activities to have him do, refer to the following list. Write (or draw) some of these on cards for him to choose. I usually had my pre-schooler choose three tasks (e.g., listen to a tape, play with Lite Brite, sort items by color) from his "Carson Can." He had a separate shelf of supplies from which to choose. By giving him the first assignment, he feels special rather than "left over." He is actively involved (at least for a few minutes) and you are fresh to start out the day's work for your older children.

The following activities not only reinforce skills but can be done independently. They are merely a sample of the kinds of activities you can "assign" your toddler.

Observing and Exploring Skills

Water play (squirt bottles, measuring cups, boats)
Sand play (measuring cups, castle molds, construction toys)
Magnets
Magnifying glass
Colored cellophane
Masking tape
Flashlight
Bubble-blowing

Verbal Development

Learning Bible stories
Dramatizing Bible stories
Learning nursery rhymes
Being read to
Answering questions about stories
Imitating speech
Naming animals
Naming parts of the body
Naming objects in the house
Dramatizing verbs such as "eat," "hop," "brush," "smell"

Visual Discrimination Skills

Classifying obects by color
Dropping a clothes pin into a bottle
Pegboard
Legoes
Lite Brite

Mr. Mighty Mind
Felt shapes

Auditory Discrimination Skills

Listening to tapes
Speaking and singing into a tape recorder
Playing "Go and Get" (Give a sack to a toddler and say, "Go and get a truck." As he
gets older, ask for several more specific items, like "Go and get a red fire engine, a
blue station wagon, and a white ambulance.")

Relationship/Measuring Skills

Distinguishing between
 Left and right
 Up and down
 Yes and no
 Go and stop
 Fast and slow
 On and off
 Short and long
 Small and large
 Rough and smooth
 Light and heavy
 Past, present, and future
Bathroom scale
Measuring tape
Measuring cups

Matching Skills

Concentration (Memory Game)
Lite Brite
Puzzles
Dominoes
Lottos
Pictures of food cards to match cans of food

Sequencing Skills

Arranging Cuisenaire rods from shortest to longest
Arranging coins (or cars, or rocks, or leaves) from smallest to largest
Arranging Dominoes from least to most

Classifying Skills

Sorting laundry
Sorting toys (e.g., vehicles, building materials, stuffed animals, books)
Sorting silverware
Sorting groceries
Sorting an assortment of household objects by color, shape, or function
Sorting magazine pictures into categories (e.g., fruit, animals, cleaning supplies)
Sorting animal cards into categories (e.g., dogs, cats, birds; pets, wild animals; adults, babies)
Sorting coins, buttons, leaves
Sorting Cuisenaire rods, numbers, letters

Creative Expression Skills

Puppet show
Googles (i.e., "Make a picture from this shape.")
Painting (e.g., watercolors, sponges, string, fingerpaints)
Print set
Play dough
Vegetable sculptures
Collages (e.g., macaroni, masking tape, wire, foil, paper shapes)
Dolls
Legoes
Dress-up
Playing with trucks and cars
Clapping to music
Playing musical instruments (triangle, drums, recorder, sticks, xylophone, bells, tamborine, horn, whistle)
Singing with tapes

Gross Motor Skills

Big Wheel
Tricycle
Wheelbarrow
Shopping cart
Doll buggy
Wagon

Sandbox
Jungle gym
Ball and basket
Kicking, throwing, and catching balls
Batting a ball from a tee
Walking sideways and backwards
Building with blocks
Somersault and cartwheel
Climbing
Walking like dog, bear, crab, worm, duck, frog
Walking a straight line
Jumping
Hopping
Skipping
Galloping
Balance beam
Cardboard boxes
Window washing (with squirt bottles and squeegee)
Vacuuming
Sweeping
Dusting
Washing dishes
Folding napkins
Setting table
Wiping placemats
Polishing silver
Opening and closing drawers and cabinets
Pouring rice back and forth
Painting sidewalk with water
Carrying a chair
Hokey Pokey
Tapes with body movements
Obstacle course

Fine Motor Skills

Buttoning
Snapping
Cutting
Tracing
Sewing
Pegboards
Threading beads
Screwing on jar lids
Medicine dropper
Zipping
Tearing and pasting
Cutting and pasting
Gluing items for a collage
Coloring
Painting
Drawing on sidewalk with chalk
Threading beads
Sewing or lacing on styrofoam

<u>General Fun</u>

Cooking help
Tea party
Nature walk
Hide-and-seek
Hide the Thimble
Tag
I Spy
Mother, May I?
Ring-around-the-Rosie
Simon Says
London Bridge
Playground equipment
Grocery store
Errands

3) Plan your times of intense concentration around your toddler.

If your young one is content to play alone for awhile each morning, plan to focus energy on your older children during that time. If your toddler naps, plan focused time during that hour.

4) Create a controlled area. Make a place for him in the schoolroom bound by chairs, bookcases or whatever.Let your toddler be part of the action and yet keep away from your five-year-old's paper. We put a piano bench at the doorway so that the toddler could watch and be part yet wander.

5) Plan your toddler's day.

Plan a schedule for him, just like you would for older children. Vary the toys you give him.

6) Assign "Watch the Baby Time" for older children.

Rotate child-care assignments. It is their responsibility to keep an eye on what the toddler is doing.

7) Let your toddler have friends over to the house.

Allow your toddler to visit with friends. Arrange a co-op just for your toddlers or invite other toddlers to join your family for field trips and other special events.

HOW DO I USE THE TIMELINES?

Each KONOS CHARACTER CURRICULUM volume has a corresponding KONOS KIDS' TIMELINE. Choose the Timeline that goes with the volume you are using.

KONOS KIDS' TIMELINE FOR VOLUME I
KONOS KIDS' TIMELINE FOR VOLUME II
KONOS KIDS' TIMELINE FOR VOLUME III
KONOS KIDS' TIMELINE OF BIBLE CHARACTERS
KONOS KIDS' TIMELINE OF ARTISTS AND COMPOSERS

Do I need the Timelines to teach KONOS? No, not unless you want your child to understand history. What better way is there to teach where people fit in history than to physically place them on a Timeline and to see them displayed? These are the reasons we recommend using the Timelines:

1) **Multi-sensory learning**

   The children cut out (if they are old enough) the figures and put them on the line (tactile), see where they fit in history (visual), and review what they have learned about this person (auditory).

2) **The big picture**

   Instead of learning mere fragments of history, the children see where individual people fit within the whole scope of history.

3) **Blocks of history**

   Since the figures have identifying characteristics (e.g., paintbrush for artists, musical notes for composers, medal for Olympic champions, staff for prophets), the children can easily see classifications of people. The Bible Timeline, for example, teaches the creation, the patriarchs, the bondage and deliverance, judges, and prophets.

4) **See people living at the same time in history**

   In our fragmented education, we were taught separate subjects without seeing how the pieces interrelated. Your children, however, will learn that Squanto (American history), Shakespeare (English literature), and Leonardo da Vinci (art history) all lived at the same time.

5) **Continual reinforcement**

   Because the Timeline is kept visible to the children, and because they use it regularly they are reinforcing previous knowledge. For example, when placing Alexander Graham Bell on the line, your child will see John James Audubon and Helen Keller again. Since we keep the Timeline on the hallway wall (B.C. on the left side, Jesus over the bathroom door, and A.D. on the right side), the children see it daily as they walk to the bathroom. Sometimes they even touch it. One morning Jordan cried to Jessica, "Mommy, I hit my head right where Ferdinand and Isabella are!"

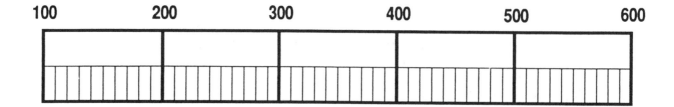

How do you use the Timelines? First place all the lines of history on a wall. Staple into sheetrock or use plastitac. Directions on how to arrange them are in each Timeline package. As you study a person, cut out the corresponding figure and place him on the line. We usually do this on Friday (review day). Ask your child to tell all he remembers about this person. As a reward he gets to place him on the line. Have your child find the correct place. This teaches him how to read dates. If he struggles, ask such questions as "Is he B.C. or A.D.?" "Is he before Jesus or after Jesus?" "In which century did he live?" "Is he before George Washington or after him?"

You may periodically remove the whole Timeline and put it back up for review. When we moved to another house we put up only the figures that our youngest son knew. That way he is starting fresh.

The Timeline figures can also be used off the lines. For example, when we studied American history, I gave Carson all the figures we had studied and had him group them into categories (Revolutionary War, settlers, government, pioneers, etc.) He then sorted them into smaller categories (Massachusetts settlers, Virginia settlers, etc.) We also played "Go and Get" with the figures. "Go and get someone who led a battle during the Revolutionary War." "Go and get the three men who warned the people of Concord that the British were coming." "Go and get someone who helped write the Constitution."

WHERE DO I GET HELP WHEN I NEED IT?

Don't panic! The first piece of advice we have is to START! Your expertise will greatly improve with experience. Don't worry if you have never taught this way. Try it and you will see where you need help.

You will greatly benefit by co-oping with other families, especially with those who have had experience in teaching the KONOS way. The KONOS Counselors can help you to locate people in your area.

The KONOS Counselors, experienced in teaching KONOS, are available to help you set up your yearly schedule, plan units, find resources, and answer your questions. They share their expertise on an individual hourly basis or in mini-seminars for a nominal fee. Call the KONOS office (214-669-8337) for counselors available in your area.

972-924-2712

BECAUSE...

Because our children are gifts from God,
Because we love them,
Because we want them to grow in godly character,
Because we want them to be fully equipped as God's people in this world,
Because we want them to be life-long lovers of learning,
We wrote KONOS.

Because your children are gifts of God,
Because you love them,
Because you want them to grow in godly character,
Because you want them to be fully equipped as God's people in this world,
Because you want them to be life-long lovers of learning,
You are using KONOS.

You have made a commitment to take the home-school JOURNEY. KONOS is the ROUTE you have chosen. This COMPASS is a tool to help you ORIENT as you PLOT THE COURSE you will take. But no matter how good the ROUTE you have chosen or how effective the COMPASS you are using, you still need a GUIDE. The KONOS Counselors are experienced BACKPACKERS, but they are only people. God is the only infallible GUIDE. It is He who is qualified to LEAD THE PACK. He, well acquainted with the TRAIL, THE ROUTE, and each HIKER, is the most effective trainer, carefully selecting what you need know and when. If you STRAY FROM THE PATH, He will leave TRAIL SIGNS for you to follow. If you need PROVISIONS, He will provide them for you.

As we have taken the JOURNEY, using the KONOS ROUTE, we have many CAMPFIRE STORIES of God's PROVISIONS for our home-school. I remember the time I fretted because of not having a music teacher. It was an obvious need, as my children were begging me not to sing to them. I finally asked God, believing that He cared for the specific needs of our family. Shortly after, my good friend who had taught music to adults for several years, mentioned her desire to teach children but to first try her methods on some "guinea pigs." Our children were the "guinea pigs." I also remember our desires for a shepherd, for a spinning wheel, for a plane ride, for a dance instructor, for a sound studio, for horses to ride, for a S.C.U.B.A. class, for free pets, for a historical trip East and for a co-op (fellow BACKPACKERS to ease the BURDEN). As we and the children prayed for these opportunities, not only were they provided but we grew in our appreciation for the Lord. Is anything too hard for our Lord? The GUIDE is so faithful.

Sometimes we do not need what we think we need (how humbling!). Instead, we may need to demonstrate God's character in the midst of afflictions. Why was it that everything went wrong during our Patience unit? The car broke down in rush hour traffic, the dog ran away, and money was stolen from us. Have you studied the Patience unit yet? We've received many letters from parents who were teaching this unit. "Our car broke down." "My husband lost his job." "You said patience is accepting the things that cannot be changed; I'm learning so much!" Here again we need to trust the sovereign GUIDE's faithfulness.

Are you ready for an ADVENTURE? As you take this EXCURSION, remember that "the journey of a thousand miles begins with a single step." Get started on the TRAIL, remembering that you are not alone, "BECAUSE He interecedes for the saints according to the will of God" (Rom. 8:27). Join us in proving that the GUIDE is good.

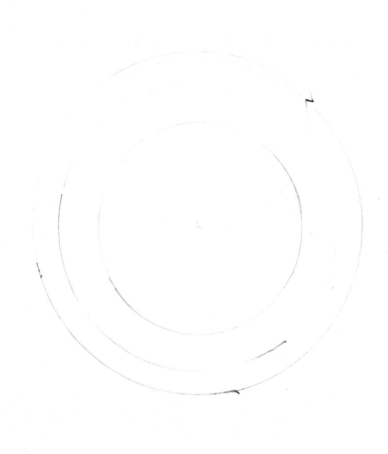